MW01140955

# Mind Games

## *Daily Meditations for Great Golf*

**Second Edition**

**William Chandon, Ph.D.**

ISBN: 9781661075217

## Dedication

To my soul mate, Bridget Fahy Chandon.

# Contents

## Acknowledgments

Steve Benson has been a terrific friend, colleague, and coach for many years. Gerry Nadler, Ph.D., has been an inspiration and a tremendous source of knowledge about the link between thinking and doing. My sister, Melissa Chandon, has been generous with her artistic support and encouragement. Thank you, Ron Lewis, for all of your superb editing. I want to add a special thank you to Ben Britt, Bill Arbour, and Mary Howlett for some extensive editing and feedback. My talented clients have taught me many powerful lessons about how fascinating athletes are and what's possible.

Thank you to some notable reviewers who gave me invaluable feedback, including Sid Roberts; Fr. Steve Hess, S.J., Ph.D.; Dave Albanese; Martin Gonzales, PGA; Dick McDonough; Doug Prazak; Dennis Paquette; Mike Bieluwka; Phil Perello; Mike Breedlove; Bob Funk; Ron Mitchell; Norman Schneider; Bill Lucas; Larry Kattner; Peter Buentello; David Palmer; Bruce LaRue, Ph.D.; David Munday, PGA; Bruce Olson, PGA; Chris Rowe, PGA; Elizabeth Wendt; Casey Heath, PGA; Layne Ricks, PGA; Wright Zimmerly, PGA; John Hankey; Ty Chamberlain; and Jeremy Pierce.

Ganesh Palapattu, M.D., was a tremendous source of healing and understanding. Lori Raijman and Isaac Raijman, M.D., engaged my imagination.

I have learned invaluable lessons over the years from my regular playing partners, including Matt Blackmon, Craig Matthew, Rick Page, Brian Rains, Boyd Robertson, Steve Parino, Steve Hitchcock, JR, Gary Lew, Gordon Wong, and Charles Miers.

Thank you, *Texas Links Magazine*, for providing a forum for me to share some of my ideas. Thank you Houston Amateur Golf Association, Memorial Park Senior Group, Roseville Golf Club, Jersey Meadow Senior Group, and Houston Senior Travelers League.

Moe Norman inspired me with his approach and his love for the game. Thank you to my swing coaches Bob Epperly, PGA; Graves Golf Academy; and Matt Swanson, PGA. I appreciate Manuel de la Torre, Michael Hebron, and Leslie King for extraordinary insights about the golf swing.

# Notes on the Second Edition

Through the process of writing the series of *Mind Games* books, I have learned some valuable lessons and refined my approach to how I present the ideas and techniques in my books. The primary goals of the second edition are to make the book simple to use and powerful to practice. I have updated the Introduction by adding an assessment to help golfers figure out what parts of their mental game need work. I have also simplified the Introduction, by eliminating some of the background information about me, which is available on my website. I have changed or updated a number of the meditations for clarity. I have also simplified the affirmations, which makes the meditations easier to practice. I have updated and simplified the meditation techniques in the Introduction and Meditation Scripts chapters. I have refined and expanded the way I use the sanctuary meditation technique. I also updated the language in the book to make it more conversational.

# *Introduction*

There is a crucial difference between reading about our mental game and improving our mental game. Having knowledge is useful, but it isn't sufficient to cause change. We need to apply our essential knowledge to make important changes and develop ourself so that we can have the golf game we desire. This book gives you a powerful way of bridging the gap between knowledge and effective actions. In meditation, we discover our essential knowledge and strategies for applying the knowledge in our golf game. We learn how to manage our thinking, emotions, and physical states in effective ways as we live our dreams.

The essence of a strong mental game is the ability to manage our thinking, emotions, and physical states in order to perform at our highest levels. We learn to manage our thinking, emotions, and physical states by practicing the right kinds of meditation. This book will coach you in how to do that.

For many of us golfers, playing at a high level or "in the zone" is an unpredictable event. We don't know when or why it happens. After we have learned to meditate effectively, we recognize that the experiences that we have while meditating are similar to the experiences we have while playing in the zone. That's because playing in the zone is a meditative state. We can learn to play in the zone more often by learning to meditate in the right ways. When we learn to meditate, we learn to manage ourself in ways that are conducive to optimal performance.

I wrote this book because, as a golfer, I have felt the need for it for a number of years. I believe a "mental game boot camp" is essential to becoming our best. Once we become somewhat proficient in the mechanics of golf, the breakthroughs happen when we develop a strong mental game. The idea of daily meditations was in part inspired by people I have known who committed to daily readings to maintain their sobriety. In addition, I have also practiced daily meditations of the spiritual genre for years. I have found daily meditation is a terrific way to center myself and have the life I want. Meditation is an excellent way to take charge of our life and develop as an athlete and person.

We can identify a meditative state because the analytical part of our mind quiets down, and we connect with the imaginative part of our mind. When we are in a meditative state, we connect with our subconscious mind. When we're dreaming, we're deeply in a meditative state and in touch with our subconscious mind. Our subconscious mind holds the keys to the breakthroughs in our mental game. We need to learn to listen to and communicate effectively with our subconscious mind.

I assume readers have no experience with meditation. The meditation techniques that we use in this book may not be what you expect they will be. This form of meditation isn't difficult to learn. It doesn't require sitting for hours in silence. This form of meditation is active and engaging. In as little as 15 minutes per day, golfers can make significant inroads on developing their mental game.

This book is for people who are serious about actualizing their potential. Development of a strong mental game takes time, practice, and persistence. Development of a mental game is similar in scope to the development of a physical game. We must consistently work on the right things in the right ways. There are large breakthroughs possible, but often it's about doing the right work and being patient for results to come.

## The Ego and the Self

The primary purpose of meditation is human development. By meditating, we're developing our thinking, emotions, and physical states to be in service of our purposes. Think of the last time you had a fantastic round of golf. You can still remember it clearly. A part of you had the experience, and part of you noticed you having the experience. In fact, since you remembered the experience, you're still noticing the experience.

We aren't our experiences. We aren't a round of golf. We have these experiences. The part of us that notices the experiences, evaluates the experiences, and forms attachments to the experiences is our Ego. Our Ego wants to keep us safe, successful, and secure in the world, while protecting us from what's "out there." Our Ego wants things to remain stable, safe, and predictable.

The part of us that recognizes that we have an Ego is our Self. Our Self is the deeper part of us that we find in meditation. In meditation, when we go deeper, we quiet our Ego's voice for a while and pay attention to our Self's voice. Our Self wants us to change, grow, mature, challenge assumptions and boundaries, have breakthroughs, and be healthy and free. By practicing regular meditation, we connect more intimately with our Self's energy so that we can push, stretch, and remove boundaries that keep us from being our best.

## Meditation and the Human System

The human person is a system. What happens in one part of the system affects the other parts of the system. As we meditate and explore the links between mind, body, and emotions, we understand our human system more fully. We understand ourself from a powerful perspective as we develop a powerful way of being in the world. We learn that we have many choices that we can make that shape who we are and what we do.

One of the most elegant aspects of being human is that as we develop ourself mentally, emotionally, and physically in our sporting lives, we begin to see shifts in the other aspects of our lives. Even though the focus of this book is on improving our golf game, by regularly practicing the right kinds of meditation, we see shifts in how we show up in our families, relationships, spiritual lives, work lives, and our communities. Being in the zone applies to all of life, not just sports.

I don't make meaningful distinctions between the various techniques that are useful to reach a meditative state. There are many effective techniques such as motivational speeches, art, retreats, concerts, novels, poetry, silence, nature, music, movies, plays, religious ceremonies, hypnosis, neuro-linguistic programming, yoga, massage, spas, and exercise. All of the experiences can help us move into a meditative state, where we still the analytical part of our mind, and we activate the imaginative part of our mind.

# Using the Book

I have grouped the meditations by month. Each month has a different theme. Each day of the month has a unique meditation. Each meditation has some thoughts for your reflection and has a unique affirmation at the end of the meditation. An affirmation is a sentence that we use to engage our imagination as we meditate. We read the meditation mindfully and meditate on the affirmation. The affirmation helps us focus as we meditate. Reading a meditation and meditating on the affirmation can take as little as 15 minutes.

Think of this book as being similar to going to the gym. Our desire is to develop our mental, emotional, and physical states, to perform our best. That takes dedication and commitment. Sometimes meditating may seem like work. Other times it seems easy and simply flows. Once we get beyond the basics and start to progress, meditation is usually simple and thoroughly enjoyable. After some time to develop the habits of our meditation practice, it becomes an indispensable part of our life.

Consider the following guidelines to help you use the book:

- Use the table of contents to get a feel for the different topics covered by the book.
- Do the meditations for the most powerful results, rather than simply reading them.
- Although I organized the meditations by month and day, you can use them in any sequence you want.
- You can ignore the dates and start with a chapter of meditations that interests you and applies to you right now.
- Some people may prefer to choose meditations randomly without concern for the day or topic.
- Stay with the same meditation for as many days or weeks as it seems worthwhile to you.

- For highly motivated golfers who are looking for faster progress, meditate several times per day using the same meditation.

## *Where to Start*

If you decide to ignore the dates of the meditations, and you're unsure of where to begin your meditations, you can do the following assessment.

Complete the following sentences as spontaneously as possible with as many endings as possible. Record your answers for further reflection.

- The things that frustrate me the most with golf are...
- My goals for golf are...
- The things that I don't know about the golf mental game are...
- With golf, I wish I could...
- I feel that I could be so much better in golf if...
- The hardest parts of golf for me are...
- I feel the least confident with golf when...
- My goals for working on my mental game are...
- I have the most fun with golf when...
- With golf, I fear...
- I know I could play better golf if...
- If I knew I could become highly skilled at golf, I would...
- If working on my golf game could help me solve problems in other areas of my life, I would want to solve...
- The things I would love to improve are...

Reflect on your answers and take note of the answers that have the most energy for you. Rank those responses according to what's most pertinent to you right now. Then use that ranked list and go through the table of contents, finding the chapters and the meditations that address those issues. That will give you a good starting point for beginning your meditation practice. You can keep returning to this assessment from time to time to get fresh perspectives about what to work on next in your meditation practice.

## Monthly Summary

The following is a summary of the monthly themes in the book.

*January: Being On Your Way*

Golf takes us where we need to go and teaches us about the world and ourself. We learn to understand golf as a journey and not a destination.

*February: Being Proactive*

We're the ones to accept the responsibility for choosing the paths we believe to be the best. We learn how to create a plan for our success.

*March: Being Triumphant*

The barriers that we have in golf are the same ones we have in life. Our barriers are exactly what we need to help propel us forward in our journey in golf and life.

*April: Being a Champion*

There's a champion inside us all, just waiting to be more present and more powerful.

*May: Being In the Zone*

The zone state is a meditative state. To play in the zone more often, we learn how to meditate in the right ways for golf.

*June: Being Powerful*

Golf has the potential to draw us into the depths of ourself, where we discover who we can be in golf and life.

*July: Being in Training*

The goal of practice is to work on the right things in the right ways and leave time to pursue other things in life along with golf. Great practice is a choice that we repeatedly make.

*August: Being a Free Spirit*

When we are a free spirit, we honor our uniqueness and find our own paths to greatness. The goal of any authentic spiritual quest is to be free to pursue our dreams. We want to be the best that we can be in golf and life.

*September: Being Healthy*

Golf reminds us that we're both mind and body and that we have to take care of both to perform at our highest levels.

*October: Being a Great Short Gamer*

Approximately two-thirds of the shots in a round of golf are short shots. Golfers do not consistently shoot low scores without being proficient in the short game.

*November: Being a Superb Ball Striker*

Being a superb ball striker begins with owning our swing and our way of playing golf.

*December: Being Mentally Tough*

Mental toughness begins by believing that we can handle anything or learn to handle anything.

## Your Sanctuary

The subconscious mind can be a difficult concept to grasp, so I use a metaphor to make the subconscious mind more concrete and understandable. I use the metaphor of a “sanctuary.”

In the world, there are sanctuaries for people, animals, and plant life. We designate something as a sanctuary when we want to create a safe and rich environment where someone or something finds safety and will flourish. “Sanctuary” can also have a spiritual meaning. Sanctuaries can be sacred places where we connect with our Higher Power. This book isn’t a religious book, but it’s a spiritual book. We can’t help but experience our spirit when we go deep inside ourself through meditation. You can experience your sanctuary in any way that works for you.

We use the sanctuary as the primary meditative technique in this book. We use our imagination to go to our sanctuary and meditate. Each time we meditate in our sanctuary, it takes on more character and detail. Our sanctuary becomes a real place to us.

At different times in our life, our sanctuary may feel more real to us than the life we're living. We can experience this when our life isn't as deep and meaningful as the reality we experience in our sanctuary.

With the right meditation practices, we eventually carry our sanctuary with us throughout the day as we live, play, work, and train. With practice and time, we begin to live more consistently with the person we discover in our sanctuary. We go to our sanctuary to meditate, and our sanctuary goes with us into the world.

Take a few moments now and begin to create your sanctuary. Each person's sanctuary will be unique and personal. Imagine the most beautiful, peaceful, and inspiring place. It should be a perfect environment for you, having everything you want. It may be an actual place, or it might exist only in your imagination. It may be a combination of several places. It can be near a beach, in a valley, on an island, or on a mountaintop. It can be anywhere you want it to be.

Experience your sanctuary in considerable detail, imagining how it looks, sounds, smells, tastes, and feels. Everything you want is there. It's perfect and safe. It has a beautiful house where you live on the property. It's the perfect house for you, being just the color, shape, and style you want. Everything you want is inside the house. The rooms are exactly as you want. You can add or change rooms in any way, at anytime. Your house is a magical place, where you only need to imagine something happening, and it happens.

Imagine you go to a high point in your sanctuary, where you can look out and see the different parts of your sanctuary. There may be streams, fields, places for animals, places where you meditate, places where you hike, places where you get away from everything, places where you go for inspiration, and places where you can talk with anyone you want. There are also places for health and healing. There are also athletic facilities and golf courses where you practice, train, and compete. There's everything you need and want. You can create the perfect place for you.

You control what happens in your sanctuary. Only people you imaginatively invite are welcome in your sanctuary. Nothing happens without your permission.

As you return to your sanctuary through meditation, you'll see and experience new things. That's how our subconscious mind works—the more we visit and open ourself to exploration, the richer the experience.

Even though our sanctuary is a metaphor for our subconscious, the experience of our subconscious through the metaphor is quite real because the language of the subconscious is metaphor, symbol, and sensation. We enter our sanctuary and subconscious mind through our imagination and meditation. Words only matter to our subconscious if they create images, emotions, and sensations for us. That's how our subconscious mind speaks to us and how we speak to our subconscious—with dreamlike images, daydreams, emotions, and sensations.

## Learning to Meditate

You should meditate only in a safe, quiet environment where you can close your eyes and fully relax your mind and body. Meditation slows down the analytical functioning of our mind. Therefore, for your safety and others' safety, while meditating, always avoid doing tasks, such as driving, that require your analytical skills and full attention. Many people find the best times for meditation are in the morning when they first wake up or at night, just before bed.

The following is a sample meditation entitled, "You're More." We will use it to illustrate the process for doing daily meditations. We will use a meditation script for doing the meditations. The meditation script guides you through the meditation process. The process for doing a day's meditation is to read the meditation through, slowly and mindfully. After reading the meditation, you meditate on the affirmation, using the meditation script.

You'll know that you're meditating effectively when the words begin to stir your emotions, trigger physical sensations, create daydreams, and make pictures and movies in your imagination. Allow yourself some time and practice to become proficient with meditation. You're learning a new skill. Be patient with yourself.

You'll take about 5 minutes to read the meditation mindfully and 10 minutes to meditate on the affirmation. You can always take more time to meditate on the affirmation, but I designed the meditations to work in 15 minutes. Now read the meditation below slowly and mindfully.

## *You're More*

We have thoughts about who we are and what place we have in golf and the world. Most of our thoughts about who we are and what we can accomplish find their anchors in our past. The problem is that our past isn't always an accurate predictor of our future. Why should we cast in concrete our sense of who we are and what we can do, when that's not necessarily accurate or even helpful?

There are certainly aspects of our subconscious mind that we're unaware of right now. Our subconscious mind is always in the process of revealing itself to us through our dreams and meditation. There are power and wisdom in our subconscious mind, waiting to make us stronger, more confident, and wiser than we are right now.

Why limit what you think you might be able to accomplish? Give yourself room to be more than you think you might be right now. Give yourself the benefit of positive belief.

***"I'm more than I think I am right now."***

## *Meditation Script*

To begin the meditation, sit in a comfortable, quiet place, where you can close your eyes and relax fully. Take a deep breath and relax your body. Then take a deep breath and relax your mind, just as you relaxed your body. You can now double the relaxation of your mind and body by opening and closing your eyes twice.

Now, imaginatively take yourself to a place in your sanctuary where you want to meditate. It could be inside your house in your sanctuary, or it could be somewhere on the property of your sanctuary, perhaps by a stream.

Imagine how it would feel to be in that place. Imagine how your body would relax even more. Imagine what you would see, hear, feel, smell, and taste in that place. Everything is relaxing.

Now slowly repeat your affirmation for the day while your imagination makes pictures, movies, sensations, and emotions. Keep slowly repeating your affirmation for 10 minutes. If you find yourself distracted during your meditation, gently bring yourself back to repeating your affirmation. You can set a timer to know when 10 minutes have passed. You can listen to music during your meditation if you find music helpful. Soothing instrumental music tends to work the best. You can also find some meditative music that lasts 10 minutes to keep track of time.

When you finish meditating on your affirmation for the day, imagine leaving your sanctuary and returning to your present location, feeling great and ready to go on with the rest of your day or night. Take a few deep breaths, stretch your muscles, and give yourself all the time you need to feel refreshed and ready to go on with your day or night.

Use this meditation script for at least the first 30 days that you're using this book. Once you feel comfortable with this technique, you can start using other meditation techniques that you'll find in the Meditation Scripts chapter at the end of the book. Over time, you'll learn what techniques work the best for you.

# *January: Being On Your Way*

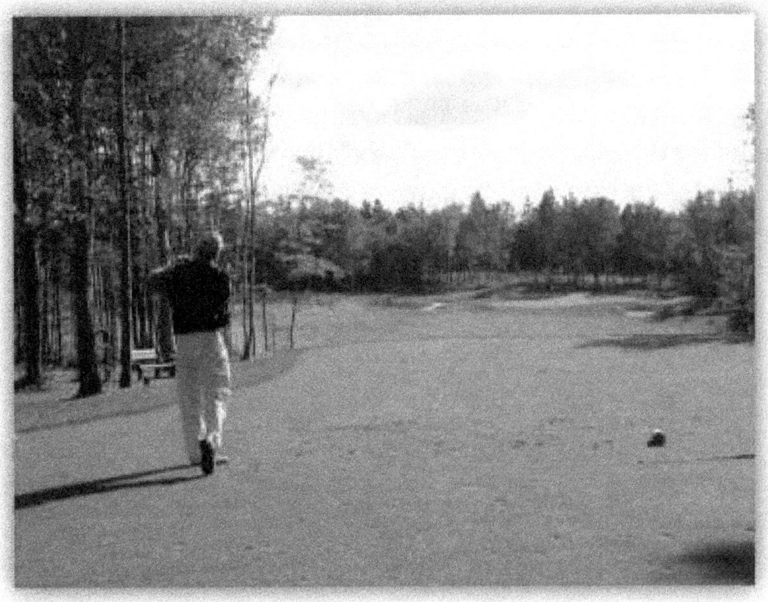

Since golf is a game that we can never fully master, we can think of golf as being a long journey. Many experiences and destinations await those of us who are willing to set out on a journey and explore what golf has for us. Golf can take us where we need to go and teach us about the world and ourself.

## January 1: The Odyssey

*The Odyssey* is an ancient and powerful story of a hero's journey. The hero leaves the safety, comfort, and predictability of home and family in order to accomplish exceptional things for the greater good. Odysseus left his home to fight in a war with Troy. He was successful in the fight, but got lost on his journey home, taking 10 years, finally, to return home. Each of the stops along the way of his return trip taught him something significant. Even though Odysseus eventually returned to his home, he was not the same person. He came home transformed.

If we take up the hero's journey in life and golf, we leave the easy, well-worn paths that others might suggest for us and seek a journey that's all our own. We look inside for confirmation that we're taking the right journey. We learn what we truly care about, and we learn about ourself. On the journey, we have successes and setbacks, sometimes getting lost along the way. We can learn some of our most important lessons when we lose our way and have to find our way home.

***"I learn from my hero's journey."***

## January 2: Daring to Be Great

We live our lives as part of social systems. Social systems prefer conformity and predictability. Things tend to work smoothly when people follow the rules, fit in, and fulfill expectations. When we're an upstanding member of a social system, it feels comfortable to be part of the system.

We don't find greatness if we hide ourself and seek simply to fit into our social systems. You must decide if you want to be comfortable and fit in or if you seek something more for yourself. Only you can choose to venture out of your comfort zone and discover how good you can be. There's no shame in being average or a decent golfer, but do you want more? To be great, you have to be different and accept that people will notice you. Perhaps you can be a great player.

***"I dare to be a great player."***

## January 3: Into Your Sanctuary

From your sanctuary, imagine that you're setting out on a hike. You're exploring more of your sanctuary in order to learn more about its power and beauty. The more you explore, the more you learn. Remember that your sanctuary can be a magical place where anything you want can happen, even unexpected, but life-affirming surprises can occur. Perhaps, as you explore your sanctuary, you'll meet some people or characters who can talk to you about going on a journey in order to learn and grow. Perhaps you'll meet other golfers along the way who will share some wisdom with you. As you continue to visit your sanctuary, you'll go deeper into it.

***"I go deeper into my sanctuary."***

## January 4: A New Journey

We can treat golf simply as a game of skill and competition. It's reasonable to do that. Golf can be loads of fun and a good setting to feed our competitive appetites. There are many lessons we can learn along the way to becoming a skillful player and competitor.

We can also view golf as a way of learning about life and ourself. We can learn how to live in ways that are more meaningful and satisfying. We can learn valuable lessons from successes and setbacks. Both experiences are in every round of golf. Golf has a way of continually asking us how we want to respond and who we want to be, both now and in the future.

***"I play golf to experience life."***

## January 5: Optimal Performance

During athletic performance, we perform optimally when our mind and body are in harmony, and the analytical part of our mind is relatively quiet. The analytical part of our mind is essential when we're in learning mode. When we're in learning mode, we're analyzing data and doing "what if" analyses. It's like driving a car in rush hour traffic. We are vigilant, prepared, and ready to react to the unknown.

During athletic performance, the imaginative part of our mind is active. It's like flying in a plane that's on autopilot. We have a feeling of being along for the ride. Thinking is straightforward and easy. It feels more like simply imagining things than thinking about things. In golf, the thinking is mostly about targets. You say to yourself, "I want to hit the ball over there." You see the target and just allow your mind and body to do what they know how to do. You're not in learning mode. You're in performing mode.

Some people take more naturally to the learning mode while others take more naturally to the performing mode. For those who gravitate more to the learning mode, their journey to high performance may feel like more of a challenge, but they can learn. Everyone can learn to play in the performing mode.

***"I play in the performing mode."***

## January 6: Confident Places

Go to a place in your sanctuary where you feel confident. The place may be somewhere that you remember being confident in the past. The place may somewhere that you imagine yourself to be in the future. The place may be an imaginary place.

When you're in that place of confidence, what do you feel, emotionally and physically? When you're in that place, how do you think? What do you do in that place? Imagine that when you're in your place of confidence, something unexpected happens. How do you deal with unexpected events when you're in your place of confidence? How do you feel about other people? How do you feel about yourself as a golfer?

Imagine going to another place of confidence in your sanctuary. Experience how it feels and how you think in that place. What do you do in that place? How do you deal with unexpected events in that place? How do you feel about other people? How do you feel about yourself as a golfer?

***"I have places of confidence."***

## January 7: Children Telling Stories

Children are natural performers and storytellers. When they get together, they can instantly create elaborate role-plays, full of adventure and suspense. Role-play is their way of setting out on a journey, setting aside the familiar, discovering new ideas, entertaining, raising questions, learning, and experiencing the wonder of life.

Similar to children's role-play, golf can help us set aside the familiar, discover, raise questions, and experience the wonder of life. Golf can take us on journeys by helping us reveal and explore parts of us that were previously unknown. We learn to find the gaps in what we know. We find that learning what we don't know is perhaps even more valuable than what we already know.

Imagine that you're a child again, and you believe that golf has magical powers to help people become wise, successful, and happy. Imagine that other children have gathered round, and all of you are telling stories about the magic of golf. Imagine what stories you and the other children would tell. Imagine what characters the stories would have. Imagine what themes and morals the stories would entail.

***"I embrace the wonder of golf."***

## January 8: More Than Winning

Some people use the language of "winning" and "losing" when they think about success in golf. That language and way of thinking can be counterproductive and lead to unnecessary discouragement. The reason is that the numbers of competitors in golf are typically large and, in the end, there's only one player with the lowest, winning score. In addition, even the best players win only a small percentage of the time. If success is winning only, then by definition, everyone else loses. Every golfer, from that perspective, usually loses.

Winning tournaments is fantastic. Finishing towards the top is magnificent. However, the most important, long-range goal is to improve and grow as a golfer and a person. If you don't play well in a tournament, what matters is that you learn something from it and move forward.

***"I'm always learning something from golf."***

## January 9: Breakthroughs Happen

Kids believe that magical things are possible or even likely. However, as we grow up, most of us give up on childish beliefs about what's possible. We learn to be more reasonable, to aim for things that are more within reach. We learn to be skeptical about breakthroughs as we grow up.

Perhaps now is an opportune time for you to let your dreams come alive again, to think and dream large, to push the boundaries of what seems achievable for you. Much of golf is about steady incremental improvements, but that doesn't mean that breakthroughs can't happen with some regularity. Our expectations can create self-limiting beliefs. What might you accomplish if you truly believed in yourself and your dreams?

***"I expect breakthroughs in my golf game."***

## January 10: Golf Plays Through You

We play the game of golf. We decide when we play, how we play, how we practice, and how much of ourself that we give to golf. All of that is true. Golf is a sport, and it serves our purposes.

If we let it, the opposite holds true. Golf plays through us. Golf is such a challenging, frustrating, and rewarding game that we can never fully master it. We act as if we're in control of our golf game, but we're not in complete control. There are times for us to try to shape our game to our own wishes, but there are also times when we can let loose and ask ourself, "What's golf trying to teach me about life and myself?" There's a place golf wants to take us if we let it.

***"Golf plays through me."***

## January 11: Everyone Is a Teacher

Many people of all skill levels are passionate for golf. Golf seems to attract interesting and engaging people from many lifestyles. How many times have you played golf as a single and joined others who turned out to be engaging and shared your passion for golf?

However, competition sometimes brings out an unflattering side of some people, even if the competition involves only small amounts of money or prestige. Some people lose themselves in competition, and it becomes more about their Ego than a friendly game.

On the golf course, whether someone is pleasant and stimulating or is unpleasant to be around, everyone has something to teach us. People can open up our eyes to things in golf that we had not considered. Others teach us things about how not to be and can be a mirror for our own behavior. Both are valuable lessons. Everyone has something to teach.

***"Everyone has something to teach me."***

## January 12: The Value of Silence

Some of us will do almost anything to avoid silence by watching TV, surfing the Internet, listening to music, texting, having conversations, shopping, or busying ourself with activities or hobbies. There are multitudes of ways of avoiding silence. Why do some of us want to avoid silence?

Silence can be a doorway to deep understanding. When we are silent for long enough, our subconscious mind starts to bubble up messages to our conscious mind. Sometimes we don't like what we hear from our subconscious mind. Sometimes we hear messages from our subconscious, such as, "I feel lonely" or "I feel unsatisfied with my life right now." These kinds of messages can scare us because they tell us that we're off course, and we need to do something about it. Conversely, it's also true that our subconscious mind can bubble up positive messages such as, "I feel good about the person I'm becoming." These kinds of messages help us appreciate where we are in life.

Taking the time to be silent is a pathway to deep wisdom and self-understanding. There are times when golf can invite us into silence. We don't have to fill up every moment in a round with conversation. We can learn to appreciate the silence between shots.

***"I appreciate silence."***

## January 13: Your Authentic Self

Our Egos sometimes want to protect us from painful truths about ourselves. At times, we can feel as if we're playing parts in movies. We can feel as if we are a collection of characters and stories that we repeatedly play. We may enjoy some of the characters and stories, but we may also be deeply weary of other characters and stories that we play.

As we become more familiar with our sanctuary, we come to find a more accurate picture of ourself, both the positive and negative aspects of us. Through meditation, when we're in touch with our Self, we begin to feel that we're finally real. We no longer feel compelled to play roles we don't want to play.

Our journey in golf and meditation helps uncover hidden parts of us. By going deep inside and exploring what we care about and what we believe, we can bring our Self more into the light of day.

***"I'm aware of my Self."***

## January 14: Learning to Listen

Wisdom begins with the acknowledgment that we don't know everything. We learn that it's fine to lack answers, even if we're intelligent people.

Acknowledging that we don't know everything opens us up to listening. Sometimes the most insightful thoughts are things that we have repeatedly heard, but we weren't listening.

Who do you need to listen to more regarding your golf game? Who causes you to think? Who creates wonder for you? What part of yourself do you need to listen to more?

***"I listen to others and myself."***

## January 15: Trusting Your Journey

There's wisdom in life if we let it unfold. Not every single event makes sense, but the patterns of events often encourage our growth, health, expansion, and freedom. Our job is to participate as much as we can in the unfolding.

Consider where you are in life and your golf game right now. Who and what events have brought you to the place that you are right now? What were some of the unexpected events that caused a shift in your life and golf game? What keeps you from trusting that your journey is a good one and that you can trust the inner wisdom that guides you along the way? What do you need to let go so that you can move forward?

***"My journey is taking me where I need to go."***

## January 16: Being and Doing

There's a difference between being and doing. Being precedes doing. We decide who we want to be as people and golfers inside our sanctuary. Then the "doing" in the world happens in ways that are consistent with our being. Some golfers, who want to change how they play, mistakenly believe that changing what they do will cause a shift in who they are as a golfer. When we do that, it feels as if we're playing a role that doesn't feel natural to us. The role doesn't flow from our being. We have to work hard at trying to be someone we're not. We keep reverting to old habits of thinking and behaving.

Our being flows from what we value most and believe most deeply from the spaces of our sanctuary. As we take our journey in golf, we have choices about who we decide to be as a golfer and person. Spend some time in your sanctuary reflecting on your most important values and your deepest beliefs about yourself and golf. See if your values and beliefs are ones that you want to keep in the future. As we develop, we can change our values and deep beliefs. We do that in the spaces of our sanctuary in meditation.

***"I'm clear about who I am and what I do."***

## January 17: Wonderland

*Alice in Wonderland* is a fantastic children's story and a powerful story for adults as well. It's a story of a girl who finds a strange new world "underneath" the normal world that most people experience. The world underneath represents the subconscious mind, the part of us that seems hidden and mysterious. Alice learned that life was not what it seemed to be on the surface. She learned to navigate the strange ways of the world below the surface. Although it was strange in the world below, her experiences filled her with wonder.

If your life seems a bit too familiar and filled with too much routine, then a visit to wonderland is in order. As adults, we enter wonderland by getting more in touch with our sanctuary through our meditations and dreams. Our meditations and dreams show us how to break the routine and inject new perspectives into our life. Perhaps something new about your perspective on golf will open up for you.

***"I visit wonderland through my meditations."***

## January 18: New Experiences

If we do the same things that we have always done, we will continue to get the same results we've always gotten. How much value is there in repeatedly practicing the same swing on the range if it's fundamentally flawed? How much can we expect to accomplish by taking the same mental approach to golf, when the approach is fundamentally flawed?

If you seek some new results in your golf game, you have to do something differently. Seek new experiences, new ways of doing things, and new ways of thinking about things. Don't be afraid to experiment and see what you can learn.

***"I embrace new experiences."***

## January 19: Being a Wizard

If we take the stories of wizards symbolically, wizards are a symbol of people who have discovered their own personal power. They operate from a different set of rules and perspectives because they have looked deep inside themselves for the truth about who they are and what they can do. What others accept as unchangeable laws, the wizard sees as a way that people explain why they can't do some magical things.

We go deep inside to discover our wizard's perspective by regularly meditating. We discover that we're stronger and wiser than we thought. We're free to start living a magical life in which golf becomes a vehicle for self-expression and discovery.

***"I'm a wizard on the golf course."***

## January 20: Your Own Vision

Sometimes we can feel that there's no one who fully believes in us or who understands our vision and dreams. Visions and dreams are highly personal and even deeper than we understand with our conscious mind. We care about things for complex reasons. We don't know all of the reasons. Our visions and dreams evolve and unfold themselves to us.

Allow your visions and dreams for the future to evolve and unfold. There's no need to cast them in concrete as if that were some sign of strength or wisdom. The nature of dreams and visions is symbolic, not necessarily literal. Do you dream of being a champion golfer? There are many ways of being a champion golfer. Find your own way to express what's most personal and meaningful.

***"I follow my vision for golf."***

## January 21: Trusting Yourself

As we become more aware of ourself in our sanctuary, we begin to see that there are consistent patterns that we can trust. Once we get more in touch with our sanctuary, a deeper logic emerges.

Our vision and our journey become clearer, and our strengths and weaknesses become more apparent.

Deep wisdom from our sanctuary helps us decide between passing fancies versus deep desires. Hence, we can make better decisions about what serves our purposes and what doesn't. With each solid decision we make, our trust in ourself increases. There's less need to second-guess our decisions. We become clearer and more decisive.

***"I trust myself."***

## January 22: Quieting the Critic

A critic lives inside most of our minds. The critic is all too quick to point out our shortcomings and mistakes. The critic says things such as, "You're not good enough," "You don't deserve to succeed," and "Your dreams are unachievable."

Part of the joy of being an adult is that we can decide what internal conversations to have. We don't have to listen to the voice of the critic if we choose not to listen to it. When we practice meditation, we learn to quiet down the various internal conversations that go on seemingly nonstop. The more we develop the ability to center ourself in our sanctuary, the more we can quiet down unwanted internal conversations.

Imagine you sit between two people who are both talking to you. One is the critic. The other person is someone who always has encouraging things to say to you about the journey that you're taking. Both people are talking to you, but the critic is loud, and you can't hear the words of encouragement.

Now imagine that you have a dial that you use to control the volume of people talking to you in your sanctuary. Now slowly turn off the volume of the critic to where you see his or her lips moving, but no sound is coming out. All you can hear are the words of the encouraging person as he or she talks to you.

Keep practicing this meditation until you can manage your internal conversations. You may need to come back to this meditation for an extended period. This skill translates to a powerful ability on the golf course. You'll be able to manage your internal conversations in ways that are helpful for you.

***"I easily quiet the internal critic."***

## January 23: Your Deep Coach

Coaches can be helpful because they can provide different perspectives for us to consider. The best coaches know their players well and treat them as individuals. They know that we're all unique in significant ways.

When we learn to go deeper with meditation, we discover that there are deep sources of wisdom available to us in our sanctuary. We discover that we have our own deep coach inside our sanctuary. As we deepen our meditations, we begin to find sources of wisdom that are particularly useful in guiding us because they come from deep inside of us and are deeply personal. The wisdom that comes from deep within knows you better than you know yourself at a conscious level.

***"I hear my deep coach's wisdom within me."***

## January 24: Internal Resources

In our sanctuary, we find a wealth of internal resources. Internal resources are the memories and beliefs that we have about the world and ourself. Internal resources are valuable because they can provide emotional encouragement and can be a plentiful source of wisdom. We all have a multitude of internal resources available to us.

Some people don't recognize their internal resources because their internal resources have slipped into their subconscious mind. It's as if they have forgotten them. We can recover our internal resources by meditating in our sanctuary.

Suppose, for example, you felt discouraged about the lack of progress in your golf game. What should you do about it? To gain access to some of your internal resources, go to a place in your sanctuary and reflect on times in your life when you felt discouraged about something. Just allow the memories to float up to your imagination. This isn't an analytical task. It's an imaginative experience. When some memories have come to you, reflect on how it felt to be in that state of discouragement. Reflect on what you did about it and how you moved past it. Reflect on the strength that you have inside of you that helped you resolve the situation. Reflect on what you learned. Reflect on what the experience changed in you. Now imagine bringing those same internal resources more into your golf game.

***"My internal resources give me strength and wisdom."***

## January 25: Staying Awake

Ironically, success can have its own challenges, just as failure can. Failing at something is highly motivating. Failure can be painful. We want to avoid failing as much as we can and move on from it as fast as we're able. Success, on the other hand, tells us that we did something well and that the approach we're taking is working. Success can become addictive because it feels so good to succeed. Most of us would like to live in a perpetual state of success.

However, there's a potential danger with success. We can fall asleep with success. The assumption we can make with success is that we simply need to keep doing what we're doing, while expecting that our success will continue forever. The problem is that the world around us is constantly changing. We're constantly changing. What works today might not work tomorrow in the same way. Staying successful requires continued course corrections. We stay aware of what's changing around us. We stay aware of how we're changing physically and mentally. We stay awake.

***"I'm awake on my journey."***

## January 26: Learning Discernment

Golf requires many decisions, both as we plan for and play golf. Sometimes small decisions can have far-ranging impacts. Is there a way of judging whether a decision is likely to be a good one before we experience the impacts of the decision?

Learning to be discerning about our decisions is a way of making higher quality decisions. We can learn to be discerning by listening deeply to ourself, learning to hear that voice of deep wisdom within our sanctuary that's steady, strong, and wise.

Reflect on some decisions that you've made in the past, ones that turned out positively, and ones that turned out negatively. Notice the differences between them. Reflect on the differences in terms of your values, your emotions, and the voice of wisdom that you hear in your sanctuary. Imagine in the future, being able to decide your course of action quickly when necessary. You now recognize the qualities of the decision and the voice of wisdom that you hear deep within yourself.

***"I make good decisions."***

## January 27: Learning to Be Quiet

Being quiet means being able to slow down our mind, which is a formidable task for most of us because our minds are highly active in modern society. We live in complicated social systems. Technology is beneficial, but it has created the need for highly active analytical minds to be able to function effectively. The analytical part of our mind is becoming highly developed. The problem is that many of us do not know how to quiet our analytical mind.

We can learn to quiet down the analytical functions of our mind, but it takes practice. In fact, it takes meditation. We need our analytical abilities, but we have to manage them and use them sparingly on the golf course. There's a fine line between enough analysis and too much analysis on the golf course. Many golfers overuse their analytical ability and underuse their imaginative ability.

***"I'm quiet when I choose."***

## January 28: Keeping Your Dream

All lengthy journeys have ebbs and flows to them. A journey with golf always has ebbs and flows. Sometimes it seems that we're making substantial progress. Other times it seems that we're running in place or even going backwards. If we accept that we will have ebbs and flows, we won't make the low points harder than they need to be. We won't assume something is wrong and that we need to do something differently.

At the low points, it's easy to be discouraged. At those times, our confidence can lag, and the clarity of our dreams can fade. Our dreams seem out of focus. It's at those times that we need most to go inside our sanctuary and reaffirm that our dreams represent what gives us passion, hope, and energy to keep going on the journey. We keep practicing when improvements seem slow in coming. We believe in our dreams even when we feel we are going backwards. Dreams that have carried us through the hard times become the most treasured of possessions.

***"I reaffirm my dreams about golf."***

## January 29: Finding Home

Home is a place where we should feel the best—supported, safe, energized, and loved. Home doesn't have to be a physical place. Home can be other people. Home can be an emotional place, an imaginative place, or spiritual place. Being on a long journey requires us to come home regularly to recharge and get ready for the next phase of the journey.

If you don't feel that you have the home that you want, the first step is to imagine what an ideal home would be for you. Imaginatively go to your home in your sanctuary. Make it exactly what you want it to be, having all of the people and things you want. What would help you feel the best, supported, safe, energized, and loved?

Anytime you want, you can return to your imaginative home. Every time you do, it will become more of a home for you. Over time, you can work to create the physical sense of home that already exists in your sanctuary.

***"I know what home is for me."***

## January 30: Your Backyard

We take journeys to discover, learn, test, enjoy, and experience life. Golf is that way too. We have to leave the safety of what's comfortable and familiar for that, which is new and probably uncomfortable, at first. We can learn and experience many things, perhaps some of which are useful at the time. Sometimes there are powerful lessons we can learn about what isn't true or useful. Sometimes we understand only after some time passes. One proverb tells us that, "A person travels the world in search of something, only to return home and find it in his or her own backyard."

In golf, perhaps the answers that you seek are already "in your backyard." Perhaps the answers you seek are something that you learned from an instructor years ago but have forgotten. If you're unsure of the answers you seek, then it's a terrific time to begin with questions. Without clear questions, the answers we seek may be right in front of us, but hidden because we don't know specifically what we seek.

What are the questions that you bring to golf? What do you want to know? What do you want to experience? What do you want to test in yourself? What do you want to discover? Perhaps the answers are closer than you know.

***"I'm clear about what I seek."***

## January 31: It's the Journey

In golf as in life, there aren't many permanent destinations. We tend not to rest in the destinations for too long because, when we reflect on it, the thing we seek most is the journey.

Suppose, for example, a golfer has a goal of having a single-digit handicap. To reach that goal, she works hard on driving the ball more accurately and works hard on her short game. It may take a while to reach the destination of being a single-digit handicap. Then one day she looks up her updated handicap and finds it's a single-digit handicap. Eureka! It feels good to have reached that destination. Perhaps she revels in the accomplishment for a month or two. If she truly loves golf, not soon after reaching a single-digit handicap, she will be wondering how she can reach a low, single-digit handicap.

That's the nature of journeys and destinations. In reality, it's always more about the journey than any one destination.

***"The journey continues."***

# *February: Being Proactive*

Everyone dreams of having a meaningful life. Dreams become real when we summon our courage, create a plan, and take action. Taking a journey without a plan is like navigating with a map that points the way in all possible directions. We're the ones to accept responsibility for choosing the path we believe to be the best. No one can do that for us.

## February 1: Your Purposes

Our purposes direct our focus, thinking, and action. Purposes are similar to values in that they help us know what we desire, so we can make consistent choices. Purposes are different from values in that values are general in nature, whereas purposes are specific. For example, we might value competition and have a purpose of becoming a successful amateur or professional golfer.

People play golf for all sorts of purposes. Complete the following sentences as spontaneously as possible with as many endings as possible. Record your answers for further reflection.

- Once I have become the best golfer possible for me, I will accomplish...
- When I dream about me being a skilled golfer, I dream about...
- If I could achieve anything I set my heart on in golf, I would...
- The things that excite me the most about playing superb golf are...
- If I were to stop playing golf right now, I would...
- The things I'm proudest of in golf are...

Assemble your list of responses and see if you can arrange them in order from largest and most important to smallest and least important. You can use your answers to help you create a vision and plan for golf.

***"I'm clear about my purposes for golf."***

## February 2: Freeing Yourself

Planning is about freeing ourself to practice the right things in the right ways. Practicing freely means that we are acting in a way that serves our purposes. Being free to practice well doesn't mean that we go to the golf course without any idea of what we want to do and what we want to accomplish.

Practice takes planning. Great practice has defined tasks and outcomes in mind. We do our best to do the things that we believe will deliver us the outcomes we desire. Sometimes we achieve the outcomes in practice and sometimes we don't. Whether we always accomplish our desired outcomes isn't essential, but we use our experience in practice to make modifications to our plan when needed. We're always learning and bringing that knowledge back to our planning process.

***"I'm free to practice in the right ways."***

## February 3: Being Systematic

The enemy of making real progress can be simplistic thinking. The antidote for simplistic thinking is systems thinking, which considers something from a number of points of view. One effective way to do systems thinking is to create a "mind map."

Take a sheet of paper and write down all the words that pop into your mind when you think about planning and improving your golf game. Write down as many ideas as you can without worrying about where you're writing them on the page. Just brainstorm ideas about planning and improving your golf game. Once you've done that and filled up the page as best you can, notice connections between ideas. Draw an arrow on the page between any ideas that connect with each other. You can write down a word or two on the arrow describing what the connection is between two ideas.

Of the connections between ideas, notice the ones in particular that seem like a new or central idea. Also, notice the connections that seem more emotionally powerful to you. Further, pay attention to the connections that require your attention for planning. Use your mind map to ensure you've planned for all the important tasks you need to consider.

*"I see and feel the big picture for improving."*

## February 4: Finding Your Swing

Part of planning in golf is deciding how we're going to swing our golf clubs. You can choose a method based on general principles. This method has a good deal of variability in terms of how a golfer implements the method, based on individual needs. Instructors who use this approach begin teaching a student based on what he or she already does.

Another method uses a highly structured approach to learning a swing. Instructors who teach this method aren't interested in what a student does currently. They want the student to swing the club their way.

Either approach can work. The key is to pick a method that makes sense to you and then stick with the method. The worst thing we can do is to treat swing methods as a buffet from which we select a bit of this and a bit of that. Worse still is to mix the two different kinds of swing methods.

It may take some experimentation to find what method feels like the best fit for you, but once you've found a method that fits, stick with it and give it a chance to work. Swing methods often take a long time to implement before they pay their true dividends.

*"There's a swing for me."*

## February 5: Planning for Nerves

One of the most common issues that golfers face is nervousness. Nervousness affects players at every level, from beginners to the most seasoned professionals. Learning to manage nerves takes planning. It should be a central part of our mental game plan.

There are different approaches to managing nerves. One is gaining experience in situations that cause us nervousness. You can practice in those situations, or you can compete in those situations. For example, if you struggle with water hazards, you can go to courses with water hazards and play and practice there.

Another approach involves using our imagination. Perform regular meditations about the situations that cause you to feel nervous. Imagine becoming highly competent and confident in those situations.

Still another approach is to practice meditation techniques on the golf course in situations where you feel nervous. You'll find many techniques in this book that you can use on the golf course. Meditation techniques that involve breathing are particularly effective.

If dealing with nervousness is an issue for you, create a plan to work on it regularly. Work on the issue until you feel your nerves are manageable in these situations. You can learn to manage your nerves.

***"I manage how I feel."***

## February 6: Imaginative Plans

Get a clear sense of how you want to practice and play in the future. Focus particularly on how things would look and feel.

Complete the following sentences as spontaneously as possible with as many endings as possible. Record your answers for further reflection.

- As I think about my best future in golf, the pictures that come to mind are...
- As I think about my best future in golf, the movies that I see in my imagination are...
- As I think about my best future in golf, the emotions that I feel are...
- As I think about my best future in golf, the physical sensations that I feel are...
- As I see the images of my future in the golf, the colors that stand out are...
- My future in golf is like...

As you review and reflect on your answers, pay attention to those that draw your strongest emotional reactions.

***"I see and feel success."***

## February 7: The Next Breakthrough

For players who have been golfing for a while, improvements are mostly incremental. The changes are often subtle and take some time to be noticeable. However, breakthroughs in golf can happen. They would happen more often if more golfers had the expectation of having breakthroughs. Often, we're our own barrier to making the progress we could be making.

To think about planning for breakthroughs is mostly a matter of using our imagination. From your sanctuary, think about a part of your game that could use significant improvement. Imagine that in the near future, you've had a breakthrough in that part of your game. How would that change things for you? How would it feel to have that skill in your game? What would you want to work on in your game after that? What would happen if you had another breakthrough in your game after that? How would that change things? Keep focusing on the next breakthrough after the next breakthrough after the next breakthrough. This process gives you a different perspective about both the present and future.

***"I have breakthroughs in my golf game."***

## February 8: Knowing Your Values

Values help us make good decisions. Values tell us what's important to us and what isn't. Values are especially useful when we're trying to decide between reasonable alternatives. Knowing what we value most is like always having a powerful GPS device, so we never lose our way.

The following are some common values for golfers. Add any that are missing for you. Then rank the values from most important to least important.

| | | |
|---|---|---|
| Achievement | Fun | Performing |
| Challenge | Growth | Relationships |
| Competition | Health | Relaxation |
| Enjoyment | Improvement | Socializing |
| Excitement | Learning | Spirituality |
| Exercise | Money | Success |
| Family | Nature | Travel |
| Friendship | Peace | Winning |

Now reflect on significant decisions you've made regarding golf. Note which decisions aligned with your values and which decisions didn't. Notice if your values have changed over time regarding golf.

As you think about your plan for becoming the golfer you dream of being, check that your plan and your values align with each other.

***"I'm clear about my values."***

## February 9: Setting Goals

Using our imagination for setting goals is a powerful meditative practice. Imagine you're pursuing and achieving goals in a three-year time frame. How would it feel? What would you be doing? How would it affect how you think about yourself and your golf game? Imagine you're pursuing and achieving goals in a two-year time frame. Reflect on how that would look and feel. Imagine you're pursuing and achieving goals in a year. Reflect on how that would look and feel.

***"I see and feel how my goals fit together."***

## February 10: Involving the Right People

No person takes a golfing journey alone. No one has all the skills and knowledge required to be successful. Successful people have supporting casts that have helped them become the people and players that they are.

Some of us don't want to depend on others because we feel weak when we do. Others of us are uncomfortable asking for help because we don't want to impose on others.

If you feel uncomfortable asking for help, imagine that you're in your sanctuary movie theater watching yourself on the screen. Imagine that you're watching yourself ask for support from someone, so that you can have what you need to be the golfer you want to be. Imagine you're feeling strong and confident. You're standing tall and are willing to do what it takes to achieve your goals.

Now imagine you're seeing images of people on the screen who can help you achieve your goals in golf. Imagine how you might ask them for help, feeling confident about asking. Imagine what you might do for them in return for their generosity.

***"I ask for the support I need."***

## February 11: Planning to Improvise

A good plan tries to eliminate the unknown and surprises as much as possible. We want steady, predictable results, knowing what we're doing and when we're doing it. Even more crucial, we know why we're doing what we do, and we have expectations of progress.

However, surprises will occur as we develop our golf game. Improvement is often unpredictable. We have breakthroughs. We have injuries. There are times we find ourself in a slump. When these things happen, we deal with them as best we can. We improvise. Sometimes, when the unexpected happens, the best reaction is just to laugh and appreciate that life isn't always predictable.

***"I improvise when necessary."***

## February 12: Preparing for a Tournament

Often, when players think of preparing for a tournament, they think of making sure their swing is just right and that they are sharp with their short game. To prepare physically is central, but only a part of the necessary preparation. We need a more comprehensive approach because we're a combination of physical and mental capabilities.

To prepare for a tournament mentally is to create an approach for the mental aspects of the tournament. The mental game is a combination of analytical and imaginative thinking. The analytical part thinks about the specifics and logistics of what we need to do to play well. We could consider such things as the kinds of shots to hit, the terrain, the required clothing, and travel if required. There are hosts of details to manage. That's an analytical activity.

In addition, there are imaginative activities that we manage as part of the planning process. You imagine yourself playing well at the course you'll be playing. You imagine hitting the shots and putts required to succeed. You imagine being confident, having fun, and performing in the zone. You imagine dealing with challenges. You prepare your mind to be ready to compete at your highest levels.

***"I prepare fully for tournaments."***

## February 13: Succeeding

To gauge whether we're making progress, we need to have more than a feeling of making progress. Having the feeling that we're making progress is helpful, particularly for fostering confidence, but having objective data helps us to be unbiased.

You want to have objective measures for the key areas that you're trying to improve. You don't need objective measurements for goals because either you achieve a clearly stated goal or you don't. It's a "yes" or "no" answer to the question, "Did I achieve my goal in the time frame I chose?"

You want to have objective measures for the actions you're taking to achieve your goals. For example, if you have a goal of becoming a scratch golfer within two years, you want a number of measures to ensure you're progressing. If putting is one of the things that you're working on to become a scratch player, you could measure such things as putts per round, putts per greens in regulation, or the number of feet of putts made during a round.

Based on your goals and your plan, what measures will help you know that you're making the progress that you desire?

***"I measure my progress against my goals."***

## February 14: Golf and Community

We're at our best when we're part of a community of people. There's a balance between personal accomplishments and being a contributing member of a community. For some, the primary community that they connect to is family. Good families keep us grounded by encouraging us and by being honest with us. They usually know us better than most anyone and help focus us on the things that matter the most. They know when we get away from the things that make us our best.

For professional golfers or amateur golfers at the higher levels, golf can become an obsession. We can eat, sleep, and dream of golf. Golf can become an unhealthy obsession if we don't balance golf with other interests, especially being a thriving member of a community. Being part of a community helps keep golf in perspective. We understand that a poor tournament or even a poor year in golf isn't the end of the world. Having no interests outside of golf is a formula for frustration and a sense of isolation. We put too much pressure on golf to be the centerpiece of our fulfillment. It doesn't have to be that way. We can have both a passion for golf and life outside of golf.

***"I have community and golf."***

## February 15: Getting Feedback

If you're truly fortunate, you have people in your life who will tell you the truth as they see it, even if it's difficult to hear.

Having people who can give us straight talk about our golf game is invaluable for creating a reasonable and honest game plan for improvement. There's certainly a need to have people in our life who are consistently positive and supportive. However, there's an equal if not greater need to have people in our life who will point out the things in our plans that seem at cross-purposes with what we're trying to accomplish.

If you could have access to one person to give you advice, who would that be? What might she say to you about your plan to improve your golf game? What might she say is missing? What might she like about your plan? If you can't meet with that person, imagine that she is with you and imagine what she might say to you.

***"I seek feedback on my plan."***

## February 16: Feedback to Yourself

Part of becoming more self-aware is the ability to be objective by providing feedback to ourself about our plans for golf. Our imagination is highly skilled in providing feedback. When we use our imagination and go deep inside of ourself through meditation, we find a deep source of wisdom that's always available to us.

Go deeply into your sanctuary, where you find your center, and you relax. Imagine that there are two chairs facing each other. Your present self sits in one chair. Your future self, who is an older, wiser version of you, sits in the other chair. Discuss your plans for golf with your future self. You might consider the following questions.

- What do you like best about your plans?
- What needs more thought?

- If you succeeded with all of your plans, what will be after that?
- What might be missing from your plans?
- When you think about yourself succeeding, how does it feel?
- What challenges might you need to overcome to get you where you want to be?
- What do you appreciate most about who you are and what you're trying to do with golf?

***"I give feedback to myself."***

## February 17: Understanding Change

Improvement in golf is often about making a number of small changes. There's often a gap between making a change and seeing the results of the change. In addition, small changes can accumulate over time, providing both unexpectedly positive and unexpectedly negative outcomes. Because none of our paths is certain, our journey with golf is always a series of experiments, finding what works and eliminating what doesn't.

Look back on your golfing life and notice what changes took longer than you thought they might. Notice the changes that proved beneficial and the ones that didn't. Notice the changes that have proven to be the most powerful. Notice how you learned your most valuable lessons in golf. Notice what changes took the most time to prove valuable. Notice what changes took the least time to prove whether they were valuable or not.

Learn to recognize what things might change quickly and what things might change slowly. See if you can learn to discern what types of changes will be beneficial and what types won't. Learn to recognize how you learn.

***"I pay attention to changes I make."***

## February 18: Right-Brain Planning

The right side of our brain is the imaginative part—the part that loves stories, images, and sensations. Our imagination is essential for creating a solid plan for golf. Imagine practicing in the future—how that might look and feel.

- Imagine what you would be practicing.
- Imagine what sorts of tournaments you might play.
- Imagine with whom you might be playing.
- Imagine that you've improved significantly and how you might have accomplished that.
- Imagine many years from now and what golf might be for you at that point in your life.
- Imagine that you've achieved even more than you dreamed was possible and how you might have accomplished that.

***"I use my powerful imagination to plan."***

## February 19: Left-Brain Planning

The left side of our brain is the analytical part—the part that figures out how things work, why things work, understands things in sequence, makes lists, and compares and contrasts things. The analytical side of our brain is essential for a complete plan.

One effective way of planning with your left brain is to do a SWOT analysis. SWOT stands for strengths, weaknesses, opportunities, and threats. Analyze your plan by doing a SWOT analysis—by identifying the strengths, weaknesses, opportunities, and possible threats to accomplishing your plan for golf. After you've done the analysis, adjust your plan by maximizing the strengths, reducing weaknesses, taking advantage of opportunities, and dealing with possible threats to your success.

***"I rely on my strong analytical ability."***

## February 20: Working Backwards

A great way to plan is to define the end goal, and then work backwards, step-by-step to the present. The closer the step is to the present, the smaller the step should be. As you plan for many months or many years into the future, larger, more general steps are the most practical for planning purposes. You don't want to spend too much energy on planning distant activities with meticulous detail. There will almost surely be changes to your plan over time.

What are your key goals? What are the key tasks that you need to do to work backward from your future goals to the present?

***"I plan from my goals."***

## February 21: Creating Checkpoints

One of the best ways of regularly evaluating a plan is to create checkpoints where we examine our plan and our progress. We often create checkpoints according to time frames. Some common time frames are monthly, quarterly, biannually, annually, three years, five years, and longer.

We can also create checkpoints based on key events or milestones. Some examples are specific tournaments (such as a club championship), birthdays, graduations, and family milestones. What are your checkpoints for evaluating your golf plan?

***"I create checkpoints to evaluate my progress."***

## February 22: Fear of Planning

Some golfers don't plan because they engage in magical thinking about improving their golf game. Others don't plan because planning honestly would require them to be explicit about their goals and fully commit to following their dreams. Still others don't plan because they fear the disappointment that will result if they don't fulfill their dreams. Still others don't plan because they fear they aren't good enough or could ever be good enough to satisfy their aspirations.

It's true that we may have disappointments along the journey in golf. That's the nature of following our dreams. Some things turn out the way we plan and some things don't. What matters most is that we set out on our journey in earnest, fully commit, overcome fear and hesitation, and give our best effort. At a minimum, we will grow as human beings, have some exciting times, and have the satisfaction of knowing that we didn't stand along the sidelines when we could have been in the game. We might even accomplish our dreams.

***"I plan confidently."***

## February 23: Your Passion

Passion is like the North Star for deciding what direction to take in life and golf. Passion fills us with energy and motivates us. Passion tells us that we care about something deeply and will give our all to following where it leads. A plan for golf lacking passion is suspect in terms of accomplishing its goals.

Reflect on your golf plan. What gives you passion as you think about practicing? What gives you passion as you think about competing? If you don't feel passionate about both areas of your plan, it's time to inject some passion into your plan.

Reflect on your past. When you felt passionate about something, how did that feel emotionally? How did it feel physically? How did it look? How did it affect your thinking? How did it affect your behavior?

Reflect on your future in golf and imagine feeling as passionate for that as you've felt passionate about other things in life.

***"I connect deeply with my passion for golf."***

## February 24: Deciding

There are many decisions we make while creating a plan. Higher quality decisions usually make for higher quality outcomes. Decisions are easier for some people than others. People want differing amounts of data before deciding. Analytical people typically want lots of data, including conversations with trusted people before they decide. Intuitive people typically want less data and may require only a gut feeling in order to decide.

Reflect on some of the key decisions that you've made in the past. Identify decisions that resulted in satisfactory outcomes. Identify decisions that resulted in poor outcomes. How did you decide? Did you require lots of data and analyses? Did you require a smaller amount of data, relying more on intuition in order to decide? Did you involve others in the decisions? How long did it take you to decide?

The best approach for deciding weighty decisions is to seek a balanced approach. Whatever your preference is, you should trust it because you've made good decisions in the past.

However, see if you can find a balance in your decisions. Try some new approaches to making decisions and expand your ability to make high-quality decisions.

***"I make high-quality decisions."***

## February 25: Solutions After Solutions

Golf is a thrilling game that invites us to master the physical and mental elements of the game over many years. The journey of golf, if we have good health, can last for a lifetime. We never stop learning or seeking to improve our ability to hit pure shots and putts. Contrast golf with other sports, such as gymnastics and football, which have a short lifespan, and we can see that the challenge of planning for golf is much greater.

One good way of planning that accounts for the long span of our golf game is to think of "solutions after solutions." Skilled planners think in terms of solutions after solutions. Solutions after solutions are a series of solutions, one following the other, and building on the previous. Contrast this approach with those who aren't so skilled at planning. They tend to think of one main solution or end. Skilled planners go beyond that and want to envision many solutions, followed by many more solutions. The solutions never have an end. If we're fortunate with good health, that's the nature of our journey in golf—solutions after solutions, after solutions.

What are your solutions after solutions, after solutions? See if you can envision a series of many solutions building on each other. See how many sets of solutions you can create.

***"I create many solutions after solutions."***

## February 26: Uniquely You

There's no one correct approach to finding what will bring out the best in each of us. We're all unique in the ways we think and feel. There's no one else who has a body exactly like ours. We're also unique with our experiences. No one else is close to having our same experiences.

Because we're unique, there's a challenge to each of us as we plan our journey in golf. Ultimately, we have to find our own way of achieving our dreams in golf.

As you consider your plan for golf, see if you can list 20 ways in which you're unique and see if you can figure out how that may make your journey in golf uniquely personal for you.

***"I'm unique."***

## February 27: When to Replan

Some people enjoy planning. They may be tempted to plan in too much detail. They may be tempted to keep tweaking their plan and not focus enough on executing their plan. For those who dislike planning, the challenge will be to provide enough detail and update their plan often enough.

There's a balance between planning and doing. We don't want to become obsessive about planning. Nor do we want to avoid updating our plan. One way to avoid both problems is to create a plan to replan. Determine the appropriate time to re-examine your golf plan, taking stock of progress, and updating your plan. Since golf takes time to develop, you should give yourself enough time to develop, practice, experiment, and improve.

Consider replanning on a quarterly, biannual, or yearly basis. You should choose a time frame that's appropriate for how much you practice and play. For those who practice and frequently play, quarterly replanning may be the best option. For those who practice and play infrequently, yearly replanning may be the best option.

If planning isn't something you do well, imagine becoming more skilled at planning. Imagine you've learned to enjoy planning. Imagine developing the motivation and skills to do a thorough job, while enjoying the experience. Imagine that the plan you create opens the doors for you to become the player you dream of being.

***"I replan skillfully and confidently."***

## February 28: Doing Into Planning

Experience can be a great source of wisdom. The key that unlocks the wisdom of experience is learning. If we can learn while we gain experience, then we begin to tap into our own wisdom. If we simply gain experience without learning from the experience, then we're wasting a precious source of wisdom. We can use the wisdom we gain from our experience to reexamine our golf plan. We will likely confirm some parts of our plan and confirm the need to revise other parts of our plan.

Complete the following sentences as spontaneously as possible with as many endings as possible. Record your answers for further reflection.

- The part of my golf game that seems to be responding the most because of my planning is...
- I have the most confidence in parts of my plan because...
- The things I wonder about in my golf game are...
- The things that might be missing in my golf plan are...
- What others seem to be noticing about my golf game are...

- I have my doubts about...
- I'm curious about...
- I hope that...
- I need to fix...
- What's working best are...

Sort through your answers and highlight the ones that cause you the most surprise, curiosity, or strongest emotional reaction. Then use the highlighted items to determine whether you need to modify your golf plan.

***"I learn from what I'm doing."***

## February 29: Planning Into Doing

A great plan without acting on the plan is as ineffective as not planning at all. The central task after planning is to get into action. A good plan will have enough detail so that we will know what sorts of activities need to occur by week and even by day for some players.

The secret to getting the most from a planning experience is to do something daily, even if that task is exceedingly small. You can take practice swings. You can practice mentally. You can meditate. You can practice putting almost anywhere. You can practice chipping in many places. You can always do something.

Examine your plan and find things to do daily that move you in the right direction. Even if you spend only a few minutes per day, find a way to do something daily to improve you and your game.

***"I act on my plan."***

# *March: Being Triumphant*

Everyone has barriers to being their best. The barriers, rather than being a problem, are precisely the things that help us move forward and have accomplishments that are worthy of our efforts. Golf and life intersect. The barriers that we have in golf are the same ones we have in life. That's the challenge and opportunity of golf.

## March 1: Clearing Out the Attic

Our subconscious mind is like an attic. If we have lived in a house with an attic for a long time, there's likely going to be a lot of "stuff" in the attic. We may not even remember what's up there.

When we're young, we pick up ideas like a sponge. We pick up ideas from family, friends, school, television, and the Internet. Mostly, children are undiscerning about what ideas they store in their mental attic. As we age, we become more discerning about what ideas we store in our attic. With time, our attic becomes a storehouse of ideas, some worthwhile and accurate and some not. Even though the ideas are in our mental attic, they still guide our behavior, like invisible maps, even when the guidance is incorrect.

Meditation gives us access to our mental attic so we can sort through what's there and root out the stuff that's no longer true or useful.

You can begin to explore your attic by completing the following sentences as spontaneously as possible with as many endings as possible. Record your answers for further reflection.

- I grow weary of thinking...
- I grow weary of feeling...
- The things that I don't trust about my attic are...
- Some unhelpful things that might be in my attic are...
- The things that I'm doing in my golf game that aren't working are...
- The things that I just can't seem to fix about my golf game are...
- The things that scare me about my attic are...
- If I were to clean out my attic, I might want to get rid of...
- It discourages me when I think about myself as...
- It discourages me when I think about others as...

Go through your answers and find the beliefs about yourself and the world that underlie your answers. For example, suppose you answered, "I grow weary of thinking...that life is hard all the time," then the belief that underlies your answer is "Life is hard all the time." For each answer repeat the following phrase until the energy of your response lessens. "I let go of my belief that... (Your response)." For example, "I let go of my belief that...life is hard all the time."

***"I clean out my attic."***

## March 2: Focus on the Beginning

We can become obsessive about results in golf, winning tournaments, lowering handicaps, and shooting career scores. It's good to dream about accomplishing meaningful things in golf. We should revisit our dreams about golf on an annual or semiannual basis. Our dreams help us to stay connected to our passion and love for the game.

On a daily basis, the focus should be on what you can start to do right now that could have a positive impact. If you're in the middle of a round of golf, the focus shouldn't be on the previous holes played, whether you played them well or poorly. The focus shouldn't be on the remaining holes. The focus should be on what you can start to do and do well, right now. Excellent performance doesn't begin in the past or the future. Now is the only time when excellent performance begins.

***"I focus on performing well right now."***

## March 3: Being Unique in Golf

To be truly free is to live in harmony with who we are in our center. When we're free, we express ourself in the world in ways that honor our uniqueness. When we all honor our uniqueness, we're like a giant jigsaw puzzle that fits together in intriguing patterns. Individuals don't lose themselves when they come together in ways that appreciate the fundamental uniqueness of us all.

Play golf in a way that fits you. If that means that you're a tenacious competitor, that's great. It's also excellent if you play only for fun, exercise, and the social side of golf. If you're passionate, play with passion. If you're fun loving, then play that way. Play in a way that honors who you are. You'll find a way that feels the best to you.

***"I play golf my way."***

## March 4: Dream Bigger

A deep part of us longs to achieve meaningful things in golf. If we go into our desire to excel in golf and sit with it in meditation, there's always something deeper and more meaningful than being a skillful golfer, although that's worthwhile.

Golf, at the depths, is an expression of a desire to live a full life. If we strip away fear, Ego and self-imposed limitations that cloud our thinking, we may start to hear our voice deep inside, which says, "Dream bigger."

***"I have big dreams."***

## March 5: Beyond the Yips

When a golfer has the "yips," he or she loses some motor control, with the resulting stroke or swing being jerky or uneven. It shows up most often in our putting, when there are fine motor skills involved. The yips come from overusing the analytical part of the brain. The yips feel particularly disturbing to some people because it feels as if parts of their bodies are out of control.

The best way to rid ourself of the yips is to use our imagination more and quiet down the analytical part of our brain. Even if you don't have the yips, it's helpful to learn how to quiet your mind while swinging a club or putting.

You can quiet your mind by focusing all of your attention on your breathing as you swing a club or putt. Start practicing this on the range, short-game area, and the practice putting green. Focusing on breathing is a powerful meditation technique that you can use as you practice and play.

You can also practice focusing solely on your breathing at home. Start by focusing completely on your breathing for a few breaths, then for one minute at a time, and then two, then three, and so on. By doing this, you're learning to quiet your mind, creating space for your imagination.

***"I quiet my mind when I desire."***

## March 6: Out of Control

Everyone has felt out of control on the golf course, particularly when learning the game. There are shots we want to hit but can't. There are putts that we feel are makeable, but we can't make them. We try to make adjustments during a round, but nothing seems to help.

Learning to be an accomplished golfer means that we're increasingly able to manage our mental, emotional, and physical states. Some days it's easier to do than others. Some days, our mind and body are out of sync, and won't perform the way we want. It happens. We're humans, not machines.

Those who have developed their mental game won't make things worse than they are. Some days, we accept that we're having an off day—we relax and flow with it. That will usually pull us out of our tailspin, at least emotionally. We may not have a superb round, but we won't make it worse by our reaction.

***"I manage how I respond on the golf course."***

## March 7: One Shot at a Time

There's a straightforward reason not letting go of past shots is an unhelpful thinking habit in golf. The reason is that the zone state manifests itself only in the present. We're present to the shot we're about to hit while playing in the zone. Everything else fades into the background. We start taking ourself out of the zone state as soon as we start to focus on things that are either past or future. Doing so engages the analytical part of our mind, which makes playing in the zone impossible.

That's why the conventional wisdom of focusing on "one shot at a time" works if we truly learn to practice it. We focus on the current shot using our imagination, rather than doing a lot of analysis about the current shot. When we give our imaginative mind the chance to focus fully on the shot at hand, we significantly increase the odds of hitting the shots and making the putts that we want.

***"I focus only on the present shot or putt."***

## March 8: Emotions and Golf

Some people play golf emotionally. Having strong emotions on the golf course is neither good nor bad as a rule. What matters is how our emotions affect us. If becoming emotional over a missed shot helps us focus and play better, then it's good. However, if becoming emotional throws us off our game, then we need to manage ourself differently.

If you're an emotional player, you want to feel the emotion, but not be stuck in the emotion. The best strategy for emotional players is to acknowledge the emotion, allow themselves a few seconds to experience it, and then move forward. Trying to ignore or bottle up our emotions isn't a helpful strategy. Emotions are like water behind a dam. The water will look for the smallest crack, and over time, the crack will widen until the dam ultimately breaks.

***"I acknowledge my emotions and move forward."***

## March 9: Playing in Fog

We hear stories of golfers playing some of their best rounds when they are sick or when they are playing in unusual conditions such as fog. Ironically, when people are in unusual and challenging situations, they are sometimes at their best because they don't have the energy to devote to trying too hard.

Their expectations don't get in the way either. They let go and play instinctively without overthinking things or creating tension for themselves by focusing too much attention on their expectations of the outcome. That's a powerful lesson to learn. Why not let go more often and play instinctively when we're not sick or in a fog?

***"I let go and play instinctively."***

## March 10: Thinking Successfully

Our analytical ability can provide lots of data and possibilities to consider. Analytical ability is essential for considering our lie, wind, yardages, club choice, shot selection, and exploring options in general.

However, what our analytical ability can't do is to imagine, inspire, and create. For example, you can inspire yourself right now by imagining yourself in an upcoming tournament or round of golf. Imagine you're playing skillfully, feeling great, and hitting all your shots and putts, just the way you want. Imagine feeling inspired to practice even more.

Your imagination is like the captain of the ship who decides the destination. Your analytical ability is like the officer steering the ship and deciding how to get to the destination at a detailed level. You need both abilities. They have their own roles to play.

***"I value my imagination and analytical ability."***

## March 11: Playing From Your Sanctuary

Playing in the zone is a meditative state with strong connections to our sanctuary. It feels a bit surreal and dreamlike because that's how our subconscious mind feels as we connect with it.

Your sanctuary is the place where you're connected and powerful. Imagine playing in your sanctuary often. Experience repeatedly how it is to play in the zone when you play in that place.

Imagine you're playing a round on your sanctuary golf course. You're playing just the way you want. You just imagine your targets, and you hit shots or putts to your targets. It's magical. You want the experience to continue without end.

With practice, you'll be able to take your sanctuary with you to the practice range and short-game area. Imagine that you're playing from your sanctuary there. Also, take your sanctuary with you to the golf course and place yourself imaginatively in the same physical and mental states that you experience when you are in your sanctuary.

Once you've meditatively lived in your sanctuary long enough, you'll be able to take it with you, and live and play from that powerful and peaceful place.

***"I play from my sanctuary often."***

## March 12: Not Caring Too Much

There's a fine line in competitions between caring about the outcome and caring about the outcome too much. It's good to want to perform well and expect to play well. However, caring too much about the outcome is unhelpful because it creates tension and poor decision-making. Playing in the zone is an extraordinarily focused, yet relaxed state of mind and body. Things are easy and have a sense of flow to them. Caring too much feels like work. It feels as if we're focusing too much energy on achieving a certain outcome.

How can you tell if you're caring too much? You can tell because you're creating tension physically, mentally, or emotionally.

***"I care without creating tension."***

## March 13: Being Your Best

Highly skilled players get the most from themselves. They take a path that's different in key respects from the approaches of others. They are always looking for a competitive edge.

Consider how you might be your best by completing the following sentences as spontaneously as possible with as many endings as possible. Record your answers for further reflection.

- What makes me unique is...
- My biggest challenges to being my best are...
- My biggest competitive advantages might be...
- My greatest concerns about competing with my full ability are...
- The parts of me that I can rely on the most are...
- The things that many people don't think about with competitions are...
- The parts of me that need development are...

Reflect on your answers and pay attention to those answers that seem to be a bit of a surprise or are more emotional than the others. Imagine in the future being the player that you dream of being.

***"I seek to be my best."***

## March 14: Quiet Mind

Our mind tends to be active like hamsters on a wheel. An active mind is adaptive in twenty-first-century living. Most jobs are substantially knowledge jobs—creating, changing, and moving information from one system to another. Having an active mind is adaptive for many jobs.

Becoming a highly skilled golfer requires you to go against the current trend of an active mind. Performing at a high level requires a quiet mind with a singular, narrow focus, which is the current shot or putt. Being present to the current shot or putt requires you to focus your thoughts, emotions, and bodily movements on a narrow task. That takes practice.

Schools don't teach a quiet mind because, at a surface level, it doesn't appear adaptive to twenty-first-century life. If learning meditation feels like a challenge, that's reasonable because meditation invites us to develop new skills. Meditation is a skill most people never formally learned in school or anywhere else.

***"I have a quiet mind."***

## March 15: Freedom to Play Great

Our imagination is the gateway to possibility. We begin to let go of whatever is holding us back when we imagine ourself being the way we truly want to be. If we can't imagine ourself being or doing something, then we can't be it nor do it.

Don't let reason or others tell you what's possible and what isn't. Only you know yourself at your depths. Your dreams can help guide you to your desired destiny. Give yourself the freedom to imagine playing superbly and being a skilled player.

***"I imagine myself being great."***

## March 16: Appreciating Barriers

It's tempting to think that if nothing stood in our way, we could have great success in golf. "If I were a bit stronger...if I were more flexible...if I had more time...if I had better coordination...if...if... if...."

However, the barriers that we have are the right ones to challenge us. Golf has a way of giving us the right barriers. The biggest barriers and struggles that we have are the exact ones that are essential for our development and learning. We can appreciate our barriers if we recognize that they are there to help us grow in the right areas. The path to growth is to accept what comes our way, but not let it determine our fate.

Some people struggle for years with the same problem. However, if we are patient, keep practicing, learning, and growing, then our biggest barriers can teach us our greatest lessons. Our greatest weaknesses can become our greatest strengths.

***"Barriers are essential for my development."***

## March 17: Unconscious Barriers

Self-knowledge opens up tremendous possibilities for an improved golf game and a higher quality of life. We don't know what we don't know. That presents a difficult problem. How do we begin to know what's unknown about us?

The first step in the process is to begin to ask questions of others and ourself. Questions such as the following are a decent start.

- How can I be more aware of others and myself?
- How can I stop limiting myself?
- What's holding me back from being the golfer and the person I desire?
- How can I be freer to be myself?
- Who can I ask about self-knowledge?
- What can I read that will help me unlock my potential?

- What meditations are essential for my self-knowledge?
- How can I be more positive and happy?
- How can I use my sanctuary more effectively to gain self-knowledge?

These are all good questions that begin the conversation within us. These are pertinent questions to bring to meditation. In meditation, we open ourself to deeper reflections that may open up areas of self-knowledge for us.

***"I'm open to learning."***

## March 18: Conscious Barriers

Some conscious barriers can be difficult to overcome, even though we're aware of them. In golf, a common conscious barrier is a lack of confidence in our ability to compete. We may lack confidence in a part of our game. We may be unable to manage our thinking and emotions, feeling excessive tension in pressure situations. We may lack clear thinking and decision-making in pressure situations. What can we do about conscious barriers?

*Imagine*

Imagine sometime in the near or distant future that you're the player you want to be. You're playing without the barrier you're currently experiencing. Continue this meditation daily until the sense of being without the barrier feels familiar and normal. In other words, when you imagine being the player you want to be, it feels believable to you that you could be that way someday.

### *Affirm*

Create an affirmation that's specific for the area that you're working to improve. For example, if you're working on being confident on the first tee, you might use something such as the following: "*I'm confident and relaxed on the first tee as I begin my round.*" Use your own affirmation in your daily meditations for as long as it feels helpful. For some difficult problems, we could use the same affirmation for a significant time.

### *Practice*

Regularly repeat your affirmation when you practice on the range or short-game area. As you practice, imagine playing superbly in the future, just the way you want.

### *Play*

When you play a round, regularly repeat your affirmation that you created. You want to make it your silent mantra that you use until the barrier is no longer a problem.

***"I use my power for change."***

## March 19: Fear

Some people play golf with fear. There are fears of hazards, out of bounds, embarrassment, shanks, yips, failure, and even fear of winning for some. If we tend to be fearful, golf will provide many opportunities to feel fearful. Fear is particularly harmful in golf because fear creates tension. Tension in golf restricts a golf swing and the touch required for the short game and putting in particular.

Fear is a natural fight or flight response. To have fear in dangerous conditions is adaptive. Without it, we might well be in grave danger. However, for golfers on the golf course, tension-inducing fear isn't adaptive. We're not in grave danger.

Refuse to allow fear to take over your golf game. If you hit a wayward shot, have a poor round, a bad tournament, or even a lousy season in golf, life will go on, and you'll get better if you keep working on the right things mentally and physically.

***"I play freely."***

## March 20: Your Private World

Sometimes what's going on outside of us can be a barrier to our performance. Sometimes conditions are distracting. Sometimes our playing partners are distracting. Other times, the importance of the round we're playing is a distraction. Distractions can also come from outside golf, things that are going on in our life that we bring to the golf course in our mind. How do we stay centered?

When we're in the zone, it feels like we're in our private world, in a different place than the other players who are playing. We feel somewhat insulated from distractions.

You can learn to place yourself in your own private world by using your imagination and practicing it with many repetitions. In your sanctuary, imagine you're playing in a future match or tournament, and you're playing just the way you want. There's a lot going on around you, but you're staying centered in your private world. Nothing bothers you and you just keep playing exceptionally.

Your sanctuary is the ultimate private world. Keep returning to your sanctuary and building a habit of being in your private world as you practice mentally. With enough repetition, you'll begin to bring your private world to the golf course more often as you play.

***"I play golf in my private world."***

## March 21: Recovering

The road back from serious injury or illness can be long and somewhat unpredictable. Some days, there's more progress than other days. Some days, on the surface of things, it feels like we take two steps forward and one step back. We don't always have control over that. However, we can always choose our attitude about what's happening to us.

Make a decision, today, to eliminate negativity from your life. Make a decision to root out negative people or influences from your life. Choose to focus on what's improving and what you can do. Even if progress on any given day seems minuscule, choose to focus on that.

We may find during recovery from a serious injury or illness that we need to seek out resources that we've not needed previously. We may need to look for support in areas that are unfamiliar. Remember that during the healing process that we're body, mind, and spirit. Take a holistic approach to recovery. Follow the advice of your healthcare providers. Feed your body healthy food. Get appropriate exercise and sleep. Feed your mind positive, healthy ideas by meditating. Perhaps read something about health and healing. Take care of your spirit by attending to its need to focus on the practices, people, and things that are deeply meaningful and fulfilling for you.

During recovery, we can still practice our mental game every day. The recovery period is a perfect time to devote more energy to our mental game.

***"I'm becoming healthier in mind, body, and spirit."***

## March 22: Ockham's Razor

William of Ockham was a fourteenth-century English Franciscan friar who proposed a rule called "Ockham's razor." Ockham's razor says that when faced with equally reasonable alternatives, choose the one that's simpler.

In golf, there are many decisions we make on the course. We consider what shot to hit, what club to choose, what yardage, what slope, how hard to hit a putt, how much break, how much wind. In addition, golf teachers take many approaches to the golf swing and golf game. Who has the best ideas? What will work for you? Of the many options you have, which ones should you choose?

In situations like these, Ockham's razor is exceedingly useful. If you have equally reasonable choices, choose the simplest. For example, if two swing coaches have what appear to be two reasonable approaches to the golf swing and one is simpler than the other, then choose the simpler one. Similarly, if you have multiple shots that you can hit from a lie, choose the simpler shot.

***"The simplest approach often turns out to be the best."***

## March 23: Resetting

When we hit a wayward shot or have an unlucky break and get angry or frustrated, we need to have a way of letting go and moving forward. We need to "reset."

Many electronic devices have the capability of resetting, to get back to factory conditions. Resetting in golf, then, is a process where we get over our anger, disappointment, or frustration so we can let it go and move forward. The more we consciously practice resetting, the easier it becomes.

To make resetting effective, you can create an “anchor” to help you reset. An anchor connects an emotion to a physical cue. For example, imagine you’re playing a round, hit a poor shot, and you get angry. Imagine tapping the back of your hand, then taking a deep breath, and feeling yourself relaxed, and ready to move forward. Practice this technique to create a strong anchor that you can use on the golf course in order to reset.

In your meditation, imagine yourself using your anchor on the golf course to reset. When you do, you’re building the brain circuitry to reset on the golf course as you play.

***“I reset and move forward.”***

## March 24: Seeing What You Want

Some golfers are naturally risk-averse. Their strategy is to try to avoid things, which is a reasonable strategy in golf because trouble is part of the game. There are water hazards, out of bounds, bunkers, waste areas, hills, slopes, and even hidden problems.

The challenge for the risk-averse golfer comes when the golfer overuses the capability of managing risk. If the only things we tend to notice on the golf course are problems, it keeps us in a fight or flight state. The fight or flight state creates physical tension and poor decision-making. We want to do only one thing—stay away from trouble.

In addition, our subconscious mind communicates in the language of pictures and sensations. If we say to ourself, "Don't hit the ball in the water," the picture that we send to our subconscious mind is the ball going in the water. Our subconscious mind doesn't understand the concept of "not" because there's no picture associated with "not."

To communicate effectively with our subconscious, we have to communicate with images that give our true intent. We have to focus on the images of things we want as opposed to what we're trying to avoid. If we want to avoid a hazard, we need to focus even more intently on the target we want to hit. That communicates our intent clearly to our subconscious mind.

***"I focus my imagination on what I want."***

## March 25: Believing 100%

Imagine how it would be if you believed 100% in yourself and your golf game. Imagine how that would affect how you feel, how you think, and what you do. Since we're all unique, believing 100% in ourself will be different from how others believe 100% in themselves.

Complete the following sentences as spontaneously as possible with as many endings as possible. Record your answers for further reflection.

- If I believed 100% in my golf game, I'd feel...
- If I believed 100% in my golf game, I'd think...
- If I believed 100% in my golf game, I'd do...
- In order to believe 100% in myself, I'm going to start...
- In order to believe 100% in myself, I'm going to stop...

Begin to believe in yourself today. Only you can choose to believe 100% in yourself.

***"I believe in myself 100%."***

## March 26: Can't Fail

The fear of failure can prevent some people from dreaming of doing positive things. It can be like a blindfold for some of us because we have magnified failure in our minds as something terrible that we should avoid at all cost.

How would it change things if the only true failures were not doing something because of fear? How would it change things if we reframed failure as a process of trying different things in order to succeed?

Fear has a legitimate role in life, which is to keep us from catastrophic error. That's a reasonable purpose for fear. Fear, however, shouldn't keep us from trying grand things because we might fail. We might also succeed. Even if we don't succeed at first, we can learn and refine our approach and try something else.

***"I see myself succeeding in golf."***

## March 27: Destined for Greatness

Some people have a sense of destiny as if there are magnificent purposes for their lives and their golf games. They have a sense that their lives matter and that they have positive things to do. Believing in a destiny of greatness is like having a spring of fresh water always running through our lives, always having a source of life and energy.

If you don't feel that way, imagine how life would be for you if you felt that you did have a magnificent destiny, a destiny of greatness. Imagine that you could achieve greatness in a way that fits you. Imagine how others would benefit. Imagine how it would feel to know that there's a grand design in the universe where you matter and your dreams matter. Perhaps those who have not felt a sense of destiny need only look deep in their sanctuary to find it.

If you do feel a sense of destiny, imagine feeling an even greater sense of destiny for your life and golf game. How would that feel? How would it benefit others and you? What would you do differently than you do now?

***"I have a destiny to accomplish great things."***

## March 28: Golf and Fun

Golf should be fun. Fun starts leaving our golf game when tension starts to gain a foothold. Tension creeps into our golf game when we make golf into something other than a game. When golf becomes more about Ego, tension creeps in and starts to erode both pleasure and skill. Even if a golfer plays professionally for large amounts of money, treating golf other than a game usually creates unhelpful pressure and tension.

Competition is part of the game. Competition creates tension only when we make the competition into something other than a way to test ourself and see how we measure up on any given day. Competition should be fun.

What if golf was always fun? How would golf be for you if you managed to have fun every time you played, irrespective of the score? How would it be to have fun in your biggest and most important tournaments? Fun doesn't create tension. Fun is an antidote for tension. If you feel that golf isn't particularly fun, then you're treating it as something other than a game. We decide what golf means to us. We all make that choice.

***"I choose to have fun with golf."***

## March 29: Starting Over

We invest ourself in ideas, approaches, and equipment in golf. Some golfers will cling to an idea, approach, or equipment long after they have stopped working well for them. The definition of foolishness is to keep doing something the same way and expect different results. It's hard to admit that what we're doing isn't working anymore because we have invested ourself in the idea, approach, or equipment.

Sometimes the hardest part of achieving something extraordinary is letting go of what we already have or do. What might happen if you let go of your current approach to golf and started over? How would you go about starting from the beginning? What would you like to try? How might things be different for you?

***"I can start over if I choose."***

## March 30: Playing Different Roles

We can think of life as being a series of roles that we play as if we were a number of different characters. Each character thinks, feels, and behaves in ways that are consistent with the character. We have mental scripts for the roles that we play. We tend to say somewhat predictable things in certain contexts. With our family, we play a role. With significant others, we play another role. With friends, we play another role. With work colleagues, we play another role. With strangers in different settings, we may play a number of different roles, depending on the setting.

The same things are true about us as golfers. We play different roles, depending on the context in which we find ourself. When we're interacting with regular playing partners, we play one role. When we're playing in a tournament, we play another role. When we're feeling under pressure, we play another role. When we're confident, we play another role. When we're feeling tense, we play another role.

Take some time and reflect on the different roles that you play in golf. Which characters would you like to play more often? Which characters would you like to play less often? Are there new characters you would like to play? Which characters would you like to stop playing altogether?

***"I consciously choose the roles I play."***

## March 31: Taking Responsibility

Some of us are hesitant to take responsibility. Perhaps we have made mistakes in life or golf that have helped create the hesitancy. Perhaps we fear being in the spotlight. Perhaps it's easier to follow others because we're not confident in ourself. We may be hesitant to take on responsibility for many reasons.

Conversely, some of us take too much responsibility. We try to control things that aren't within our control. Some of us use worry as a way of trying to control a situation.

Reflect for a few moments on how you feel about responsibility. Do you take responsibility for yourself and your golf game in appropriate ways? Could you take on more responsibility? Do you need to let go of some things that aren't within your control?

***"I take responsibility and accomplish significant things."***

# *April: Being a Champion*

There's a champion inside of all of us, just waiting to be present and more powerful in our mental game. We find our champion in our sanctuary. We seek more access to our inner champion's passion and energy to be our best.

## April 1: Clearing the Way

Confidence is like caring for a garden. If weeds dominate the garden, the good plants can't grow and mature. We need to pull the weeds and till the soil, so the good things that we plant can grow and mature.

Complete the following sentences as spontaneously as possible with as many endings as possible. Record your answers for further reflection.

- The reasons I'm not deeply confident are...
- My confidence as a golfer falls when...
- In the past, the things that have shaken my confidence the most are...
- My confidence gets low because...
- I know my confidence could increase if I just get rid of...
- The biggest barriers to feeling confident with my golf game are...
- The hardest parts of confidence for me are...

Sort your responses and find the ones that have the most energy for you. For the higher energy responses, say the following: "*I now let go of* (whatever your answer was)." Keep repeating the phrase until it feels that some or all of the energy flows out of your response.

***"I'm a confident player."***

## April 2: Being a Champion

The first thing to realize about being a champion is that champions come in all shapes, sizes, and backgrounds. We need only to look at the great men and women golf champions throughout the years. Their stories are unique, intriguing, sometimes improbable, and yet equally inspiring.

The first step to being a champion is to be able to imagine ourself being one. There are all kinds of champions, not just on Tour. That's a truly magnificent thing about golf—that golfers play competitively at all levels. There are club champions, league champions, amateur champions, junior champions, senior champions, and all levels of golfers.

You're the one who owns your dreams and aspirations. You decide how you'll be a champion and what your level of competition is. Imagine in the near and distant future being the champion of your dreams. How will you look? How will you feel? How will you act? How will you think?

***"I find a champion inside."***

## April 3: Being a Closer

Players can learn to become "closers," golfers who get better when it matters the most. Closers know how to focus more, believe in themselves more, and find deeper ability to bring out their best. Being a closer is a learned behavior for most of us.

Begin believing today that you're a closer and that as the key situations arise in a match or tournament, you sharpen your focus and get better. Start believing that you have another gear that you can shift into when it matters the most. Imagine that you love coming down the stretch of the last three holes of a tournament or match. Imagine that you're playing exceptionally, feeling skilled and confident, and not wanting to be doing anything else. Imagine how you look, feel, act, and think. Imagine you always play this way. You're always a closer, living for these moments when you show who you truly are.

***"I'm a closer."***

## April 4: Being Special

Everyone wants to be special in some way. We want to believe that there's a special purpose for our lives. It's true that we're all special because there's only one version of each of us in the world. There will never be another you. Even if it feels as if no one else acknowledges your special presence in the world, you can acknowledge it and appreciate it. Be yourself. Live and play golf in a way that's uniquely you.

Being a champion can be more than winning tournaments. There are many kinds of champions in golf. It doesn't require anyone to recognize you as a champion. You first recognize yourself as a champion. If others do in addition, that's a bonus. Consider how you're special and how you want to be a champion in golf.

***"I'm special."***

## April 5: Being Nice and Winning

Some nice people have a difficult time competing with all of their ability. They empathize with their competition and consciously or subconsciously restrain themselves. In order to compete fully, give yourself permission to treat golf as a competitive game. Winning is excellent. We can genuinely shake the hands of the people we beat after the match.

Always play with a competitive motivation. Many people like to play for a small amount of money. Even a small amount of money can be motivating. If you don't like playing for money, you can play for your favorite beverage after the round.

Find something to motivate you in every round you play. You can compete against the course, against the field, against competitors, or against your personal bests such as a score or other stats that you track.

Expect to win. Every time you tee it up, expect to play well and win. Believe that you can shoot a career round anytime you play.

Win by a large margin. We can be tempted to ease up if we are ahead in a match or tournament. Get into the habit of finishing strongly and decisively.

Sometimes it's helpful to play with a chip on your shoulder. If the last tournament you played was disappointing, let that irritate you and motivate you to play better.

Imagine winning tournaments and matches. Our imagination is powerful. Imagining accomplishing something is the first step towards being able to do it. We're unlikely to be able to do something until we have imagined it.

Have fun freeing your competitive side. You might discover some new things about yourself.

***"I'm a wonderful competitor and person."***

## April 6: Trusting Your Decisions

Golf is a game of decisiveness. For example, with club selection, if we choose a club that's okay and commit to it—that's better than the perfect club without the commitment. No amount of data will ultimately prove whether we're making the right choice about a club beforehand.

There's no such thing as 100% certainty with decisions we make on the golf course because there are too many variables to manage. The search for complete certainty in decisions leads to analysis paralysis and an overactive analytical mind on the golf course. At best, we make educated guesses about what we do. No one knows if a decision is ultimately the correct one until after we see the results. Begin today to commit to decisions with less than 100% certainty.

***"I trust my decisions and commit myself completely."***

## April 7: Training Your Brain

Studies show that mental practice dramatically trains our brain to do what we want. Those people who actively exercise their brains are up to 800 times more effective at using the part of the brain that they desire to engage. In one study, people who meditated were significantly more effective at engaging the part of the brain that creates a sense of well-being.

We can apply this idea to golf. If we practice engaging the part of our brain that activates while we play in the zone, we will find it increasingly easy to access that powerful part of our brain. "Mental practice" is a key component of improving our game. Our brain has to learn how to function in the right ways to get the best results.

***"I train my powerful brain."***

## April 8: Playing Through Pressure

Playing at a high level when the pressure is on is one of the key skills that golfers need to have. We can learn to deal with pressure. In pressure situations, start saying positive things to yourself rather than the negatives that reinforce past failures or struggles. Use short affirmations such as "*I can do this*," "*I'm gaining confidence*," or "*I'm improving*."

In addition, in your meditations, remember when you did handle yourself well in difficult situations. It doesn't necessarily have to be a golf memory. Tap into those positive memories and emotions often in your meditations. Replay those "movies" often in your mind as you meditate.

We can also manage our body in stressful situations, by practicing "progressive relaxation." With progressive relaxation, we relax the muscles in our body from head to toe. Right now, slowly scan down your body, relaxing your muscles along the way. Take at least a minute to do the progressive relaxation technique. Don't rush it. Also, remember to breathe deeply as you relax your muscles. The more you do this, the better you'll be at consciously managing your body during a round.

***"I thrive in key situations."***

## April 9: Creating Good Suggestions

"Suggestions" are part of meditative technique. Suggestions are a way of communicating with ourself at a deep level, a way to train our mind with the thoughts we want. You can learn to create good suggestions for yourself that communicate with your subconscious mind in a deep and meaningful way.

Here are the characteristics of good suggestions. Good suggestions are unambiguous and in the present tense. Good suggestions engage our senses. They also have specific, concrete outcomes, which are easy to verify if accomplished. Good suggestions have a reward for achieving them. Suggestions are similar to affirmations, except that suggestions are detailed. We use them in similar ways in our meditations.

Imagine you have an upcoming tournament, and you want a suggestion to prepare yourself mentally for the tournament. Here is an example of a good suggestion.

*"I play with a higher level of confidence than I have played in the past. I feel confidence as a feeling of relaxation in my chest.*

*I imagine myself having my best tournament of the year, and that gives me even more confidence in the future. I feel a keen sense of accomplishment."*

Now create your own unique suggestion for an upcoming tournament or match. Use your suggestion as you would use an affirmation. You might want to write down your suggestion on a 3 x 5 card or your electronic device. In addition, read your suggestion at various times during the day as you take a break from what you're doing, and imagine yourself succeeding.

***"I communicate powerfully with my mind."***

## April 10: Symbols of a Champion

In your sanctuary, imagine that you surround yourself with symbols of a champion. Symbols can be any people, objects, shapes, works of art, quotes, spiritual symbols, colors, parts of nature, and particular kinds of clothing, among other things. Imagine having a life where you surround yourself with symbols that move you to feel and think like a champion. Imagine taking a journey in your sanctuary to places where you discover new symbols of being a champion. Imagine your feeling of being a champion increasing as simple, commonplace objects become symbols of inspiration and power for you.

***"I fill my life with symbols of a champion."***

## April 11: Inner Champion

Our subconscious mind has different "characters" that we play as we live our life and compete in sports. Some of the characters are more conscious to us than others are. One of the characters is a "champion," the deep part of us that loves to compete, loves to win, and thoroughly believes in our ability. You can unleash your inner champion by developing more of a relationship with that part of yourself in your sanctuary.

Imagine you're sitting in your sanctuary in a place with two chairs facing each other. Your present self sits in one chair. You inner champion sits in the other chair. Spend some time with your inner champion, getting to know this character more, and being present to this wonderful part of yourself. Imagine that you can also see and understand yourself from your inner champion's perspective. Perhaps you'll surprise yourself with what you discover.

***"I find my inner champion through meditation."***

## April 12: The Gift of Greatness

For adults, greatness is a gift we give ourself. Others can support us and believe in us, but if we don't believe in ourself, all the support in the world won't be able to convince us that we can be remarkable in golf and life.

Complete the following sentences as spontaneously as possible with as many endings as possible. Record your answers for further reflection.

- I think to be great in golf, the things I would have to do are...
- The things that keep me from being great in golf are...
- To embrace the idea of greatness, I would have to...
- The things about being great that scare me are...
- For me, greatness in golf would look like...
- If I were unafraid of being great, I would...
- To be a great golfer, I need to start...
- To be a great golfer, I need to stop...

- To be a great golfer, I need to continue...

Look over your answers and center on the ones that have the most emotional energy. The answers will be a mix of things holding you back and things that you need to do. See what emerges for you.

***"I'm a great player and person."***

## April 13: Playing With Belief

You may not know how you're going to become your best, but you can begin today to believe deeply that you're becoming your best. Results follow belief.

Go to a place in your sanctuary where you're in touch with your past. Remember a time when you genuinely believed in yourself. It doesn't have to be in golf. It can be anytime in your life. If you don't remember a time when you genuinely believed in yourself, imagine how it might have felt to believe deeply in yourself.

Notice the feeling of that belief. Where in your body do you feel belief? Perhaps the feeling is in your gut. Perhaps you feel warmth in your chest. Now feel that feeling intensifying in a pleasant way. Imagine having that same feeling playing golf in the near future. Every time you play golf in the future, you feel that feeling and fully believe in yourself, whether you're playing well that day or not.

***"I believe in my ability to be my best."***

## April 14: Playing Against the Best

Intimidation can be a critical factor in golf. If we believe that we can't beat someone, then we almost certainly can't, even if we're a better player. Being a champion means that we want to play against the best at our level, whatever level that is. Champions look forward to the challenge of testing themselves and seeing what they can do. Champions raise their games when it means the most. They get up for the big tournaments and the big matches.

Playing against the best is also a learning experience. We learn about ourself and our game, and what it takes to compete at a high level. Champions keep coming back to compete. They learn what they need to do to compete and win.

Imagine in the near and distant future, you love to compete against the best, playing your best when it means the most.

***"I love to play against the best."***

## April 15: Selective Memory

All memory is selective memory. We subconsciously choose what we remember. Mostly we remember the extremes of experiences, both positive and negative. Those types of extreme or intense experiences are only a small part of life for most of us. The great percentage of life is rather mundane for many people—just going through routines, with some ups and downs, but mostly unremarkable.

What do we do if negative memories are taking up too much space in our consciousness? What do we do if we feel that we tend towards a negative point of view, focused too much on what didn't work and didn't turn out the way we wanted?

We can have some control over what we remember and how we remember it. Remember a time playing golf that was difficult or painful for you. Imagine sitting in your sanctuary movie theater watching a movie of the experience. Now play the movie of your experience repeatedly, both backward and forward. With each playing of the movie, slowly dim the colors and have the images on the screen start to lose focus. Keep playing the movie and dimming the colors until the screen is dark, and there is no sound.

Now do the same process with pleasant memories of golf except that you brighten and intensify the colors and clarity of the picture in a way that is pleasing to you. You can also zoom into the picture, making it larger and more vivid than before. Also, intensify the positive feelings that you felt as you experienced that pleasant memory. Keep running the film backward and forward until the experience is clear and vivid.

***"I focus on positive memories."***

## April 16: Finding Motivation

Champions motivate themselves not only to keep competing well but also to improve. There's no limit to how good they believe they can be. The secret to creating high motivation is to have a passion for something.

Passion is a deep caring and emotional attachment to something or someone. It makes things come alive and keeps life full of wonder and energy. Without passion, motivation becomes simply a matter of willpower, which feels like "work" and will eventually fade over time. As long as we have a passion for something, there's no fading of motivation over time. We simply do the things that we need to do. We seem to have endless energy for doing what we want. We take the time to practice mentally and physically because we care so much about what we're doing. We think and dream about accomplishing our goals. When we get up in the morning, we can't wait to do what we need to do to keep moving forward.

Consider what would give you passion and motivation for improving your game.

- How would your life change if you felt a much deeper passion for golf than you do now?
- How would it look if you became a highly skilled golfer?
- What would you gain from your accomplishments as a person?
- What would you gain as a golfer?
- What would you gain as a person who is part of a family?
- What would you gain as a person who is part of a community?
- What would change about the way that you feel about yourself as you grow and change over the years?
- What stands in your way of being more passionate and motivated in golf and life?

***"I have a deep passion for golf."***

## April 17: Living Your Dreams

It's easy to become discouraged with golf because it's a hard game, takes many hours of practice, and often results are slow in coming. In addition, since it's mostly an individual game, we usually don't have the support of teammates. It's up to us to keep our fire burning. That places the burden on us to be positive and always to keep one eye on the future. Keeping one eye on the future helps us know what to do in the present.

Did you have a dream for golf at one point that you abandoned? See if you can resurrect the dream in some fashion. Can you live part of the dream? Is there a different dream now or even better dream? If you made some changes, could you resurrect your dream fully?

***"I hold on to my dreams."***

## April 18: Owning Your Confidence

Golf is full of ups and downs. When we're playing well, we often feel as if we will continue to play well forever. Similarly, when we're in a slump, it often feels as if we will never get our golf game back. For most golfers, when we play well, our confidence is high. When we play poorly, our confidence is low. Confidence follows the state of our game.

However, our confidence is wholly within our control. We're the ones who decide the basis of our confidence. Most of us only allow ourselves to feel confident if we're playing well. We can change that. We need to take ownership of our confidence and take responsibility for defining the basis of our confidence.

From now on, if you're in a slump, you choose to believe in yourself, that you'll continue to work on the right things and that you'll start to play well again soon. Confidence should precede good play, not follow good play. If you're playing well, you choose to be confident that you'll continue to play well, even if your game varies from day to day or week to week.

***"I choose to be confident right now."***

## April 19: Self-Acceptance

We've all made mistakes in life and golf. We've squandered opportunities and made a mess of things at times. That's part of being human. What we do about it is what matters most. Do we continue to feel guilt and regret? It takes energy to disapprove of ourself. Guilt and regret are anchors to the past, sapping the energy we need to be our best right now. Yes, we can learn from our mistakes, and that's valuable, but to carry guilt and regret helps no one and sabotages our present and future.

Self-acceptance is a medicine that heals our spirit. It allows us to move on and apply our energy to the present and future. Being a champion requires our focus and energy. Champions who have accepted themselves have a lightness of spirit. They just seem to enjoy themselves fully and appreciate the moment. They don't need to puff themselves up with Ego. They are fully present to themselves and others, giving themselves fully to what they care about right here and now.

Self-acceptance begins today by making a decision to live fully in the present. By doing that, you can give yourself unreservedly to what you aspire to be and do.

***"I accept myself completely."***

## April 20: Feeling Appreciation

In your sanctuary, imagine that you're sitting in the middle of a circle of people. The people sitting around the circle are people you know and who care for you. They can be living or have already passed on from this life. Imaginatively, go around the circle and let them tell you what they appreciate most about you. They can talk about your connection with golf or life in general.

Feel the energy that comes from hearing how good and talented you are. Notice in what part of your body that you feel that energy. Perhaps you feel it in your heart. Wherever it is, notice it and have it grow even stronger in a pleasant way as if you were turning up the dial for more intensity. Now imagine playing golf with that same feeling of appreciation.

***"I feel appreciation."***

## April 21: Everything Is Motivation

Whether we have positive or negative experiences in any round of golf, the experiences can be helpful as long as we decide that every experience is a possible source of motivation. If we play superbly, it fuels our desire to play even better. If we play poorly, rather than become discouraged or angry, it fuels our desire to practice and play much better next time. If we choose to look at golf this way, every experience in golf is motivation to improve.

***"Every experience is motivation to improve."***

## April 22: The Right to Be Great

Do we have the right to be great? Who decides whether we have the right to be great? Can we simply decide to be a great player?

Each of us must decide if we have the right to be a great player. No one can legitimately decide that for us. Our parents can't do that. Our coaches can't do that. Our friends can't do that.

If you don't accept it and believe it, no one can convince you that you are or could be a great player. Make the decision today that you're going to be a great player, whatever your level of play. Be a great player with your regular playing partners. Be a great player at your club. Be a great amateur. Be a great mini-tour player. Be a great Tour player. It's up to you to aspire to be a great player at the level that fits you.

***"I have decided to be great."***

## April 23: No Excuses

Excuses are a way of avoiding responsibility. If the problems in our golf game aren't our own, we can never fix them because the problems are "out there." In addition, there are subconscious factors at work in excuse making. Players can subconsciously decide to lose a match or tournament. A player could do that for many reasons. Some players fear success and others don't believe they deserve to win. Some players don't think they are good enough while others fear recognition. The reasons are many.

To begin to explore whether there's subconscious sabotage at work in your golf game, complete the following sentences as spontaneously as possible with as many endings as possible. Record your answers for further reflection.

- I would play better if...
- The things that get me down about my golf game are...
- I would be a winner if...
- The things that hold me back are...
- The things that scare me about golf are...
- I could be great if...
- I will get better when...
- The reasons I'm not playing to my potential are...
- Success scares me because...
- Failure scares me because...

The best way of dealing with subconscious barriers is first to acknowledge them. Then fill your mind with positive thoughts such as the affirmations in this book as you meditate.

***"I compete with all of my energy."***

## April 24: Unending Optimism

The first thing to recognize in golf is that the ideas of winning and losing are different in golf than they are in many other sports. In football, for example, it's one team against its one opponent. It makes sense to talk about winning and losing.

Contrast football with golf. In a golf tournament, it's one golfer against many golfers. Yes, one golfer will eventually win the tournament, but for the others, it doesn't make sense to say they "lost." They finished in some place other than first, but it doesn't make sense to say that the whole field, other than one person, lost, as if playing well doesn't matter for the rest of the field.

Even great players only win a small percentage of the time. It makes more sense to look at our performance in terms such as finishing in the top 5, top 10, top 20, or top half of the field. In addition, another way of measuring performance is to compare our performance to past performances. Are we improving? If so, we celebrate that. If not, we work on the areas of our game that are holding us back.

Take the longer-term approach that sees golf as a journey of unending improvement, rather than each tournament being an end destination. We don't abandon our goal of winning, but we appreciate our performance relative to the rest of the field and relative to our ability. We realize that winning doesn't happen every time we tee it up. If we don't feel that we're losing most of the time that we're competing, it's much easier to be optimistic about our performance. If nearly every outing in golf is a "loss," that can be discouraging and disabling.

***"I consistently choose to be optimistic."***

## April 25: Feeling Good Decisions

From your sanctuary, think back to times when you trusted your decisions, and they worked out well. What was the process that you used to make the decisions? When you made the decisions, how did it feel emotionally and physically? People who are in touch with their body and emotions can feel when decisions are good ones. They may feel it in their gut or their heart area or any place in their body. Pay attention to what your body is telling you about the decisions you're making.

Now imagine how you carry yourself as the champion that you are on the golf course. Imagine playing with high levels of confidence in your decisions. You feel them in your body.

***"I recognize the feelings of good decisions."***

## April 26: What a Champion Does

Think of someone you know or have watched who acts like a champion. It could be someone in golf or some other sport. It could also be someone who is a champion in life.

Imagine that you're watching that person in your sanctuary movie theater. Notice what this person does. Notice how this person moves. Make the images even bigger, brighter, and bolder in a pleasant way.

Now imagine that you become part of the movie. Imagine you feel what your champion feels. You know what your champion knows. You do what your champion does. Now imagine you're playing golf in the near future, acting as the champion that you are, feeling yourself to be a champion and doing the things a champion does.

***"I'm a champion inside and outside."***

## April 27: Playing Well

Since golf is a game of never-ending improvement, we can get lost in the idea of improving. Improving becomes the goal and not the means to a goal. The goal of improving should be to play well.

If you find that you're working so hard on improving that you never seem to play well, then you may be lost in the idea of improving. If your game is always in flux, then it's time to slow down on the idea of improving and focus on playing well.

To play well and with consistency, we have to have a sense of playing from a consistent place, where our game is relatively stable, and we're seeking to play our best from that place.

Think of improving in golf as being like taking a trip on a train. If you stay on the train all the time, you may see some terrific golf courses as you pass by, but you won't be able to play them and enjoy them. To play great golf, you have to get off the train for a while, stay in one location, and play golf your way, to the best of your ability.

There's a rhythm to golf improvement. When you find you're becoming stagnant with your game, then it's time to improve some part of your game. When you find that your game is in constant flux, then it's time to stay where you are for a while focus on playing well with the skills that you already have.

***"I focus on playing well."***

## April 28: Champion's Warm-Up

The best approach to mental warm-up is to be conscious and deliberate with our affirmations. Develop your own positive affirmations based on things that are keys for you playing well.

As you're hitting shots, chipping, and putting prior to the round, say your affirmations to yourself. Use your imagination and imagine the feelings that come with the positive affirmations.

You can write down your important affirmations on a 3 x 5 card or your electronic device. Refer to them before your round as you're warming up. Choose one for the day to help keep your focus. You can continue to repeat your affirmation throughout your round.

This book is full of affirmations that you can use. Here are some examples of positive affirmations:

- I'm a champion.
- I love to compete.
- I expect to play great.
- I manage myself during a round.
- My body is relaxed and responsive.
- I hit my irons crisply to targets.
- I focus on making good swings and putts.
- I enjoy competing and playing like the champion that I am.
- I hit my drives to targets with confidence.
- I stay positive and enjoy playing.
- I keep my mind focused on targets.

***"I focus my mind, body, and emotions."***

## April 29: Human Systems

We are a system of mind, body, and spirit. If one part gets out of sync, it affects the whole person. We need to eat well, sleep well, exercise, and feed our mind with some good reading, music, and relaxation. We need to care for our spirit as we take time to be with other people who care for their spirit. We need to meditate to keep ourself centered and strong. A champion is healthy and strong in all aspects of his or her life.

***"I care for my whole self."***

## April 30: A Champion for Others

Being a champion for others is a precious gift that we can give to others. As we become more mature and healthier—mentally, physically, and spiritually—our focus can shift from what we need to what others need.

Others have helped us on our journey. Think about some of the people who have helped you on your journey. There comes a time to shift focus and help others on their journeys.

Even if you inspire only one person to move closer to her potential and get more out of life and her golf game, then you've accomplished something significant. You've made a difference in someone's life. Sometimes little things we do can have a substantial impact on others.

Imagine playing golf and being a champion for others. How would you look, and what would you be doing, saying, thinking, and feeling?

***"I'm a champion for others."***

# *May: Being In the Zone*

If we want to play in the zone state more often, we have to practice, just as we do with other parts of our golf game. We can learn to play in the zone more often by meditating in the right ways, both on and off the golf course.

## May 1: Comfort Zone

The comfort zone in golf is the range of scores we shoot that feel comfortable to us. If we shoot higher than the range, we feel uncomfortable. If we shoot lower than the range, we feel uncomfortable. Many factors determine our comfort zone. We are most concerned about the factors that keep us from shooting low scores.

Complete the following sentences as spontaneously as possible with as many endings as possible. Record your answers for further reflection.

- The downsides of shooting low scores are...
- I could shoot lower scores regularly if I just got rid of...
- If I could fix things that would help me to shoot low scores, they would be...
- The parts of my mental game that keep me from shooting lower scores are...
- I struggle mentally on the golf course when...
- The biggest mental errors I seem to repeat on the golf course are...
- I would be confident shooting lower scores if...
- When I start to shoot low scores in a round, I expect to...
- When I start to shoot low scores in a round, I start to think...
- When I'm shooting low scores, I don't like feeling...
- The things that usually keep me from shooting low scores are...

Sort through your answers and find the ones that have the most emotion and energy for you. Imagine yourself in the future playing freely, unlimited by your own thinking.

***"I let go of self-imposed limitations."***

## May 2: Being in the Zone

Being in the zone state is a meditative state. Just like meditation, the zone state has different levels. When we start to enter a light zone state, we start to experience our body being on automatic pilot, where it can do some complex things with ease.

When we go deeper into the zone, we feel our mind quieting down and slowing down. Our internal chatter quiets down. We can focus our attention for a long time on what we want.

When we go even deeper still, we feel somewhat disconnected from what's going on around us. Our mind and body connect effortlessly. We only need to imagine what we want to do, and we do it. We have a sense of being in a private world, similar to how it feels when we are in our sanctuary.

***"I play deeply in the zone."***

## May 3: Difficult Golf Courses

The first and most crucial step for successfully doing something is to be able to imagine doing it successfully. We imagine successfully playing a difficult golf course. Every time we think about playing a difficult golf course, we program our thinking for success. We imagine hitting the shots that we want to our targets. We imagine making our chips and putts.

It doesn't matter if you've played a course poorly every time you've played it. Your attitude is, "This time, when I play this golf course, I will hit the ball just the way I want to my targets. I'm going to hit the chips and putts that I envision. This time I will be successful." A habit of imagining success is a different way of thinking, a disciplined and optimistic approach to playing golf. You can't afford the luxury of entertaining failure. Holding a successful positive image of what you're trying to accomplish gives you a chance to succeed.

***"I enjoy playing difficult golf courses."***

## May 4: What You Feel

There are two ways of feeling. There are emotions, and there are physical sensations. Both are important abilities that help us to connect with what's going on around us. They are the equivalent of antennae in the animal kingdom. They give us information that we use to make decisions.

Next time you're on the golf course, between shots, pay attention to what you're feeling. Take some time to focus on the physical sensations you feel as you walk and play. Also, take some time to pay attention to the emotions you experience as you play. Enjoy feeling whatever you're feeling without evaluating it or creating a story about it. Let the feelings and emotions speak for themselves.

Playing in the zone has a lot to do with just noticing things and feeling things, without analyzing and telling ourself stories about what we're experiencing. When we start to analyze and tell stories about what's happening, the zone experience starts to fade.

***"I pay attention to what I feel."***

## May 5: Golf in Your Body

A well-struck golf shot is a celebration of what our body can do with clubs and a golf ball, masterfully navigating a golf course. Golf is fundamentally about doing something, not thinking about something. Thinking is essential in golf, but it all happens before we hit a shot or stroke a putt. Golf is a game played in our body, not our head.

During the golf swing, thinking will usually only get us in trouble. When it's time to hit a shot, the time for thinking has ended. Thinking during a swing leads to "playing swing" rather than playing golf. Playing swing leads to analysis paralysis, rather than being athletic on the golf course. Golf is a game played in your body.

***"I stay within the feelings of my body while I play."***

## May 6: Optimal Performance

Playing in an optimal state is something we can learn to do. We're already on the road to mastery by practicing daily meditation.

The next step is to begin to take your meditation practices to the range and short-game practice areas. As you practice physically, take time to practice mentally. Don't simply hit one shot after another. Take the time between shots to imagine playing in the near future at an exceptionally high level. Imagine yourself thinking and feeling what you want. Imagine often playing in an optimal state. You're becoming a master of optimal performance.

***"I practice and play in an optimal state."***

## May 7: Expanding Comfort Zones

The best way to change behavior is to imagine some more attractive and beneficial alternatives to our current way of doing things. Reasonable people will make the choices that bring them the greatest benefit.

However, new patterns of thought, feeling, and action take commitment and practice in order to become habits. It's like going to the gym. Each time we do it, we're investing in our well-being and creating new patterns of thought, feeling, and action. Acting on a new pathway creates momentum and confidence that something new can emerge.

***"I build new habits of thinking, feeling, and acting."***

## May 8: Staying Present

To stay in the present is to have a quiet, analytical mind. It's a state of mind and body focused on what's right in front of us. It's noticing what's going on and how things feel rather than analyzing, critiquing, or telling ourself stories about what's going to happen.

Since our mind wants to think about something, we want to give it something to think about that's likely to promote staying in the present. One effective meditation practice is simply to pay attention to your breathing. Give your full attention to how it feels in your body when the air comes in, fills your lungs, and then goes out. Pay attention only to your breathing for as long as you can. When you start, you may only be able to observe a few breaths before you get distracted. Be patient with yourself. It takes practice to improve. Over time, you'll develop the ability to stay present to your breathing for longer periods.

***"I stay present and breathe deeply."***

## May 9: Slowing Down

The analytical part of our mind usually races, jumping from idea to idea—past, present, and future. The imaginative part of our mind prefers a slower pace and likes to stay focused for longer periods on one subject. As you develop the ability to manage mental, emotional, and physical states, you'll notice that golf seems to slow down mentally. You'll stay in a meditative and imaginative state of mind for more of your golf game. Your thinking will become simpler and quieter. Your golf game will become more athletic and fluid.

***"I notice my mind slowing down."***

## May 10: Choosing Yourself

We begin to live habitually in the present when we realize that who we are doesn't depend on what has happened in the past. Who we are right now doesn't depend on who we want to be in the future. Who we are is who we choose to be right now. The next decision or action we take is the most significant in defining who we are and what we will accomplish.

Golf is about hitting the current shot. It's about being present to this moment. To do that, you have to let the past and the future go, and give your full attention to the present. Both golf and life are about who we choose to be and what we choose to do at this moment.

***"I choose who I am as a golfer right now."***

## May 11: Understanding the Past

To be alive is to have a past. Our past helps us define who we believe ourself to be, which helps us make choices in the present. Our past is the collection of stories that we retell ourself.

When we think about the idea of our "past," we realize that our past is a fabrication of our own choosing. Of all of our possible memories and experiences, we sort through them subconsciously and choose which ones we remember as our past. Most of our experiences never come to consciousness. If our memories are mostly happy memories, then we have chosen those. If our memories are mostly unhappy, then we have chosen those. If our memories are mostly unremarkable, then we have chosen those.

Rather than thinking of our past as a fact-based documentary of who we are, we can understand our past as being more fluid and open to interpretation. We don't lock ourself into an interpretation of our past that limits our present and future. The past is only the collection of stories we have retold ourself over the years. Similarly, our experiences as a golfer are the stories we retell others and ourself. Are your memories of golf primarily pleasant ones, or are they ones involving struggle and disappointment? You choose your past.

***"I'm who I choose to be right now."***

## May 12: Letting Go of the Future

In the same way that our past can be an impediment to living in the present, our future can be an impediment to living in the present. We can be mentally stuck obsessing about the future while ignoring the present. It's good to plan, but it isn't good to live in the future by constantly obsessing about it. No one owns the future. We create desirable visions of our future, let any obsession go, and live right now. Being in the zone is right now.

***"I embrace the present by letting go of the future."***

## May 13: Practicing Presence

Being present is hard for many of us. Being present is a practice that schools don't teach. In fact, we learn how to "multitask," doing many mental and physical things at one time. Multitasking may be an adaptive skill for portions of our lives, but it is unhelpful in athletic performance. For athletic performance, we need a singular focus and quiet mind.

One good way to practice presence is to focus on your senses. Simply focus on the feelings you have in your body. Slowly scan your body from head to toe and simply notice what physical sensations you're feeling. Focus your full attention on the body scan, thereby quieting your mind and narrowing your focus. Perform a body scan three times right now and during the day as you think about this meditation.

***"I'm present to what I feel."***

## May 14: Enjoying Your Emotions

The past exists only in our mind. The future exists only in our mind. There's only this moment in which we can think, feel, and act. Embrace "this moment" throughout the day, whenever you think of this meditation. Pay attention to the emotions you have as you give yourself fully to the moment. Try to avoid labeling the moment as "good" or "bad" or anything else. Just experience the moment and try not to think about it and label it. Experiencing something is different from thinking about something.

When we play golf in the zone, we're attending to the present, enjoying and experiencing the present, and not needing to fill up the moment with words and analyses.

***"I enjoy this moment."***

## May 15: Your Body's Movement

Our bodies are remarkable instruments. It's easy to habituate ourselves to the wonderful things that our bodies do for us. As you're moving around today, notice how gracefully and easily your body does what you want without having to give it explicit instructions. We don't have to tell our hands what to do when we drive a car. We don't have to tell our feet how to operate a car. We simply have an intention to turn, and we turn. We simply have an intention to stop, and we stop.

In golf, when we learn to trust our body and play to targets, we allow our body to be the most skillful. When we consciously fill our mind with many swing thoughts and ideas, we prevent our body from acting instinctively and masterfully. Golf is a fantastic way to wake up to the wonder that is our body and what it can do.

***"I'm thankful for what my body does so artfully."***

## May 16: Listening

Our mind wants to have a focus and something to do. Listening gives our mind something to do. Listening is a powerful way to be present to what's going on around us. Listening is a powerful way to quiet our mind as long as we can listen without analyzing or critiquing.

Golf is the perfect setting to pay attention to the sounds that you hear. Between shots, you can listen to the sounds of nature—birds singing, wind blowing, and trees rustling. All of these are pleasant sounds, which can soothe your mind, emotions, and spirit.

Between shots, you can also listen to the sounds around you that people make—the sound of a struck golf ball, laughter, celebration, and banter. You can listen without judging or critiquing if your intention is simply to listen.

***"I simply listen to what's going on around me."***

## May 17: Using Your Imagination

Our imagination is the doorway that opens up the possibility of playing in the zone state on a regular basis. Imagination activates the part of our brain that plays and performs. We find that part of our brain in our sanctuary when we meditate on our golf game.

The deeper we go into the part of the brain that plays and performs, the more we play in the zone state. The more we access that part of our brain, the easier it is to return to it. It may seem hard at first to access that part of your brain, but it's a skill that you can develop. After some regular mental practice, it begins to feel as a natural and normal place from which we play golf.

***"I engage my imagination to play in the zone."***

## May 18: Breathing Relaxation

Breathing is an amazing thing that we do. Without breathing, we would die within a few minutes. Breathing is also a powerful meditation technique.

Notice any part of your body that's tight or needing to relax. While you focus on that part of your body, take a deep breath, hold for a few seconds, exhale, and breathe relaxation into that part of your body. Repeat the technique until that part of your body feels deeply relaxed.

You can also practice this technique on the golf course. When you practice this technique, in addition to relaxing your body, you're keeping your focus on the present.

***"I breathe relaxation into this moment."***

## May 19: The Critic

Most of us have an internal critic who likes to point out areas of golf and life in which we're not measuring up to our standards. Some of us know the internal critic well because the internal critic doesn't stop. Others recognize the internal critic, but the conversations are sporadic. The standards that the internal critic would have us live up to are often impossibly high and unattainable. The internal critic can feel similar to a schoolyard bully, always looking to tear down and belittle, never satisfied.

There's a difference between being aware of our shortcomings and beating up ourself over the shortcomings. Being aware of shortcomings is helpful. Beating up ourself over shortcomings is unhelpful.

As we develop the ability to manage our thinking, we can decide what internal conversations we're willing to have. We can decide to turn down the volume of the internal critic. Over time, we can turn off the volume of the internal critic if we desire.

In your sanctuary, imagine there are two chairs facing each other. You're in one chair, and your internal critic is in the other. Imagine that your internal critic is saying the types of things that he or she usually says to you. Now imagine you have a volume button that controls the volume of the critic's voice. You slowly turn down the volume. The critic's voice starts to fade. You keep turning down the volume until the critic's voice fades to silence. As you look at the critic, you see the image of the critic fading. The image continues to fade until the image disappears.

Now, imagine that someone else sits in front of you in a chair. That person is someone who understands you and encourages you. See the image becoming bright and sharp in a pleasant way. Hear the words of encouragement becoming louder and clearer with time.

Keep repeating this meditation until you can easily turn down or turn off the volume of the critic.

***"I manage the volume of my internal critic."***

## May 20: You're Developing

We base our ideas about who we are and what we think we can accomplish on both the past and the future. We know what we have accomplished in the past. We have a vision of the future we want to create. We have hopes for what we might accomplish in the future.

However, our subconscious mind is always in the process of revealing itself to us. It's as if we're building a path into the present and future as we're walking on the path. We place a stone on the path and then we take the next step. Only when we have taken the next step and then the next, and the next after that, can we understand the wisdom of our journey.

You're in the process of becoming aware and developing. You're learning, growing, improving, and discovering how good you might be. You're becoming skilled at meditation. Believe that you can play golf in the zone more often than not.

***"I'm developing."***

## May 21: Shifting Your Emotions

Having awareness of our emotions and the ability to manage emotions requires development for most of us. Some people are better at managing their emotions than others, just as some people are better at managing themselves physically. However, we can develop our ability to manage our emotions. The first step in the development process is to become aware of what you're feeling at any given time.

Complete the following sentences as spontaneously as possible with as many endings as possible. Record your answers for further reflection.

- I tend to feel the happiest on the golf course when...
- I tend to feel the most fearful on the golf course when...
- I tend to feel the most frustrated on the golf course when...
- I tend to feel the most peaceful on the golf course when...
- I tend to feel the angriest on the golf course when...
- The emotions that surprise me on the golf course are...
- The emotions that I rarely feel on the golf course are...
- The emotions that I wish I had more often on the golf course are...

The next step in the development process is to begin consciously changing what you're feeling. You can do this right now by using your imagination. You can change what you're feeling at anytime by shifting your focus to something else. For example, from your sanctuary, remember the times when you were the happiest. Remember them in detail, how things looked, felt, and sounded. Enjoy remembering and feeling the wonderful feeling of happiness. Anytime you want, you can return to a desired emotional state by having your imagination take you there in your sanctuary.

***"I shift my emotional state when I choose."***

## May 22: Letting Go

Playing in the zone is more about letting ourself go into it, as opposed to trying to do something. We can't force our way into the zone. Going into the zone is like waiting for an invitation to enter an exclusive gathering. We can't force our way inside. We wait for the invitation to go inside. Becoming agitated only makes matters worse.

We also can't analyze our way into the zone. Being in the zone isn't an analytical state of mind. Analytical activity is a way of understanding so that we can control our environment, others, or ourself. We must quiet our mind and let go of the need to control things consciously by analyzing them. The zone doesn't work that way. We can't control the zone state. We must let ourself go into it.

***"I let go into the zone."***

## May 23: The Zone With Others

Golf is a social game. We play golf either in the zone or not in the zone with other people. Some people are more naturally social than others are. For introverts, being social can feel draining because it takes their energy to manage their social situation. For extroverts, being social gives them energy as they interact.

Being in the zone with other people around is more akin to the experience of being an introvert than an extrovert. We feel as if we're in our private world. We feel somewhat pleasantly disconnected from others. We can be social and interact with others, but the interactions feel easy. The interactions aren't the kinds of interactions that are likely to stimulate our analytical abilities. Being in the zone feels easy. Analysis is about dividing things—separating, distinguishing, judging, sorting, and deciding. Any social interaction that generates analytical thinking can wait until after the round.

***"I stay centered in my private world."***

## May 24: Connecting

Being in the zone is a state of connection. Our mind and body connect naturally, easily, and athletically. We don't need to "try" when we're in the zone state. We simply imagine hitting a shot to the target and our body knows what to do. Being in the zone is like tying our shoes. We don't need to tell our body how to do it. Our body already knows.

In the zone state, we connect to our clubs. The clubs feel more like a part of us than not. We also connect to our targets. There isn't a sense of "me" and then a sense of "target." Target and self connect.

To connect to something or someone, we have to be open to the connection. If we decide that we don't like playing a certain golf course or don't like playing in certain conditions, then we're not open to being in unison with the field of play. If we're not open and connected, then playing in the zone isn't possible.

***"I'm always open to whatever conditions I experience."***

## May 25: Actively Accepting

In golf, we often find ourself in circumstances that we would not consider ideal. We can have bad lies, bad breaks, and demanding shots. To play in the zone requires an attitude of acceptance of the current situation, which means the current shot. Everything else that has gone on before or will happen after the current shot is a distraction. Distractions are the enemy of playing in the zone.

Further, there's a difference between passively accepting the present and actively accepting the present. Passive acceptance is like going along for the ride as if someone else determines the direction. Passive acceptance of the present is to acknowledge that we may not like what the present holds, but we accept it and will deal with it.

Actively accepting the present means that we embrace the present moment as if we had chosen it. There's no sense of the present being undesirable. We see it as a stage on which we perform. The circumstances may be difficult or exceptionally challenging, but we accept the circumstances as an opportunity to perform our best.

When you actively accept the present, you're never a victim of circumstances. You can't perform at your highest levels if you feel yourself to be a victim of golf and circumstances. There's no reservation and no excuses. You accept the present as if you've chosen it.

***"I actively accept the present."***

## May 26: Keeping It Flowing

The zone state likes to keep things uncluttered and flowing. There's an easy and slow rhythm to our thinking and movements. The experience feels akin to sitting by a river and watching the water flow by endlessly, enjoying our sensations of sight, hearing, smell, and touch. We lose track of time. We're above the ordinary experiences of our sensations. Life becomes magical and remarkable for a while. There's a sense of feeling that life should be like this more often as if this is a natural state.

We don't need to entertain ourself with complex and insightful thoughts. Right now is all that matters. Right now is a good place to be. Thinking is secondary. Experience is primary.

***"I appreciate the flow of the zone state."***

## May 27: Walking Through Nature

Golf is a walk through nature. Nature has a beautiful way of bringing us back to our center. When we feel the wind on our skin, see the beauty of the grass, trees, and water around us, and hear the birds singing their songs, we come back to our center, where we know who we are and what we value most.

Nature reminds us that our problems aren't as weighty as they otherwise seem. She reminds us that our lives are precious gifts that we should appreciate every day. She reminds us that it's good to be human, playing golf, breathing, living, laughing, and celebrating the good things that we can do with a stick and a ball.

***"I let myself go into nature and find my center in it."***

## May 28: The Storyteller

A storyteller lives inside each of us, providing ongoing commentary about what's happening throughout the day. It's a familiar conversation. The storyteller usually tells similar stories. Sometimes we agree with the commentary and sometimes we don't. We can find the commentary irritating at times. The storyteller helps us stay conscious and aware of what's going on around us. In life, the storyteller is mostly useful. In golf, our need for the storyteller isn't as great. The storyteller activates the analytical part of our mind, which keeps us from having our mind quiet and playing in the zone state.

Meditation is a great way to quiet down the storyteller. Right now, go to your sanctuary and relax totally. You're simply noticing what's around you, feeling no need for commentary or storytelling. You're just an observer, being content simply to observe.

***"I let go of the need to tell stories continuously."***

## May 29: Zoning Into Music

Good music awakens our spirit. Good music is a meditation technique that can lead us into the zone state. The best music for meditation quiets and focuses our imagination.

Listen to some music that you find particularly inspiring. From your sanctuary, use your imagination to explore what place you want golf to have in your life in the coming months and years. Imagine that you're playing just the way you want. Imagine you're playing in the zone a good deal of time. Imagine that you've become a master of your mental game.

***"Music teaches me about the zone."***

## May 30: Silence

Silence has a way of stripping things away from us so that we can hear the voice of deep wisdom inside of us. The usual noise around us can drown out our voice of wisdom. By giving silence more space in our lives, we can hear the voice of wisdom more often.

If you've ever gone backpacking or camping, you may have experienced the internal silence that comes from being outside with no phones, TVs or other distractions.

The zone state usually feels like a "silent" experience. Even if we're in the middle of cheering fans, there's silence that comes with the zone state.

***"I have more silence in my golf game."***

## May 31: Living in the Zone

Learning to play golf in the zone is an incredible skill to have. Playing in the zone is one of the best experiences a golfer can have. The more experiences we have playing in the zone, the better it is.

A great benefit of learning to play in the zone is that we can begin to experience the zone state in other parts of our life other than golf. We are in life as we are in golf.

***"I live more in the zone."***

# *June: Being Powerful*

Competition is a powerful vehicle to help reveal the things that are holding us back and the strength and wisdom that's already within us. Golf has the potential to draw us into the depths of ourself, where we discover who we can be in golf and life.

## June 1: Need for Motivation

Motivation is different for different people. Explore how you think and feel about motivation. Complete the following sentences with as many endings as possible, being as spontaneous as possible. Record your answers for further reflection.

- When I'm motivated in golf, I feel...
- When I'm motivated in golf, I think...
- The times when I have been the most motivated in golf were...
- The times when I have been the least motivated in golf were...
- My motivation may be different from others because...
- I have felt motivated to practice when...
- I lacked motivation to practice when...
- When I lack motivation for golf, I...
- The biggest challenges for me regarding motivation for golf are...
- To get myself more motivated, I need to start...
- To get myself more motivated, I need to stop...

Pay closest attention to your answers that surprise you or carry the most emotion. These answers will help you know what you need to consider as you continue to develop your motivation for being the powerful player you want to be.

***"I understand how motivation works for me."***

## June 2: Two Kinds of Thinking

There are two general types of thinkers. One type of thinker tends to think about what is or could be. The other type of thinker tends to think about things that aren't or things they don't want. If we're an "is thinker," we will easily think about the things we want. "I want to hit this club 100 yards." "I want to be putting from below the hole." If we're a "not thinker," we will easily think about the things that we don't want. "I don't want to hit the ball in the bunker." "I don't want to hit the ball towards the out of bounds stakes."

Both styles of thinking are useful on the golf course. Ideally, however, we want to move easily between "is thinking" and "not thinking" as the situation requires. The first step toward having both capabilities is awareness that there are two types of thinking. The next step is to practice thinking with both styles of thinking, incorporating more of the style of thinking that is not natural for you.

***"I manage my thinking."***

## June 3: To Emote or Not

Golf teaches us about our emotions. Some golfers discover rage inside themselves. Some golfers maintain an exterior of calm but churn inside. Others experience little emotion on the golf course.

Common wisdom says that golfers should never get too high or too low. There's some merit to this approach because emotions can cause tension and poor decision-making. Excessive happiness or anger can both cause tension and poor decision-making. However, like all generalizations, there's always a bit of truth and a bit of falsehood in them.

Emotions are neither good nor bad in themselves on the golf course. Some golfers play well with some anger, finding themselves focused and determined. Other golfers play well when they are quiet and peaceful. Still other golfers play well when they are excited and having fun. It depends on what brings out the best from the individual golfer.

From your sanctuary, reflect on different times that you've played your best.

- What was your emotional state?
- What helped you recover after you had hit a few wayward shots?
- What emotions are most effective in focusing your attention on what you want?
- What brings out the best in you when you're in a tightly contested golf match?
- What emotions have proven to be unhelpful for you in the past?
- If you could be emotionally any way you want on the golf course, how would you want to be?

***"I manage my emotions in ways that work for me."***

## June 4: Dealing With Distractions

A part of developing as a golfer is to be able to deal effectively with distractions, including people or situations that would otherwise take our focus off what we want to do.

The core skill of meditation is focusing our attention at will and remaining focused for an extended period. Meditation is the best medicine to cure distractions. We consciously take our focus off the distraction and place it where we want. Highly skilled golfers are able to focus and maintain their focus on what they want.

You can use many different meditation techniques to deal with distractions. You can simply focus on your breathing. You can focus on soothing images such as the beauty of the golf course. You can take yourself imaginatively to your sanctuary. With practice, you'll find it easier to deal with any distraction.

Go to your sanctuary golf course and imagine you're playing a round with distracting playing partners. You decide to shift your focus onto something else. You're becoming so adept at shifting your focus that it's as if you can't even hear or see the distracting golfers. Imagine their images shrinking, being quiet, and becoming out of focus until their images become a blur. It's as if they aren't even there. You're entirely at peace in your own private world.

***"I focus my attention where I want."***

## June 5: Managing Yourself

We can develop the ability to manage our thinking, emotions, and physical states. Learning to manage our internal states and physical states is a developmental task. We have a series of tasks we learn, just like learning golf. When we first take up golf, there's a lot to learn. We don't become an expert overnight. Notice how highly skilled athletes in other sports who take up golf have to learn just like everyone else. There's knowledge and skill that they must acquire step-by-step. As we practice the right things in the right ways, we develop skill.

Golf, perhaps more than any other sport, requires that we manage our thinking, emotions, and physical states. Having poor thinking, unchecked emotions, and physical tension can quickly ruin a round. Golf is about managing ourself and doing so when the pressure to perform is at high levels.

The central pathway to learning to manage ourself is by meditation. We go inside and learn the deep knowledge required to manage ourself in ways that align with what we desire. We learn how to shift our thinking, emotions, and physical states as desired.

Go to your sanctuary, perhaps to a new place in it, where you feel you're capable of managing yourself more effectively than ever before. Imagine how it would be to play golf exactly as you want. Notice how you would think and feel, and what you would do.

***"I manage myself artfully."***

## June 6: Having More Clarity

Clarity comes when we have access to the deeper parts of our mind. The difference between knowledge that we have deep inside and knowledge that we gain from reading golf magazines is that the knowledge deep inside is personal and highly actionable. Knowledge that we have from our sanctuary is like having a sharpened knife that makes short work of the tasks before us.

Knowledge that we gain from magazines, books, or others is useful knowledge, but it has an abstract quality to it because it's someone else's knowledge that we have borrowed. For that knowledge to be useful to us, we have to take it an extra step and figure out how we can apply it to our golf game.

***"I have deep knowledge."***

## June 7: Right Brain

Our imagination provides an invitation to change and freedom. Without the ability to imagine things being different from what they are, we will simply repeat our existing patterns of thinking, emotions, and behavior. There would be no learning and no growth.

The right side of our brain speaks in the language of pictures, feelings, and sensations. The right side of our brain engages our subconscious mind, taking highly complex ideas and movements and turns them into something that our body can artfully perform. Athletic performance is substantially a right-brain activity. We just imagine doing something, and our mind and body collaborate and perform. Skilled athletes have well-developed right-brain functioning. We develop right-brain capability by meditating, both on and off the golf course.

***"I use my imagination powerfully."***

## June 8: Left Brain

Golf requires that we have good analytical skills. We make many choices about strategy, club selection, shot selection, reading greens, lie, and weather conditions. There are innumerable variables and choices. That creates the need for solid analysis and rapid decision-making.

To improve our analytical abilities, we can do two things. We can pay attention to our analytical processes, noticing what makes for good analysis and decisions and what makes for poor analysis and decisions. The second thing we can do is learn from others, how they approach the analytical parts of golf. We can talk to other golfers who consistently seem to make good decisions. We can also learn from others by reading some golf and self-help books about analysis and decision-making.

***"I use my analytical ability to make great decisions."***

## June 9: Into the Backyard

There was once a match between two skilled golfers. They were on the 18th tee with their match, all square. The hole had a row of houses lining one side of the fairway. The cagey older golfer said to the younger golfer, "Don't hit the ball into the backyard." The younger golfer became so irritated with the comment that he couldn't clear his mind. Where did the ball go? It went out-of-bounds into a backyard with a nasty hook.

This little story illustrates a vital lesson about our subconscious mind. Our subconscious mind doesn't understand the concepts of "no," "not," or "don't." Our subconscious mind works by pictures. If someone tells you, "Don't hit your ball into the backyard," what picture do you see in your imagination? You likely see a mental picture of the backyard with your ball in it. The lesson is to give your mind positive pictures of where you want the ball to go. Focus even more intently on your target.

***"I focus on vivid pictures of what I want."***

## June 10: Spirit and Golf

Think about inspiring stories of people who you know personally or through media. The stories that move us are about the human spirit and the call within to do something magnificent with our lives.

Golf can help us to do something magnificent with our life because golf teaches us about ourself. We learn our strengths and weaknesses. Golf asks us to be deeply in touch with ourself so that we can draw out the best of ourself and do our best to manage the areas where we need development. Golf teaches us to believe in ourself. Golf teaches us to hope that our persistence will pay off. Golf teaches us to be ever optimistic in the face of sometimes slow progress. Golf teaches us to be courageous when we feel down or disappointed. Finally, golf teaches us to celebrate with our whole spirit when we can feel our dreams just might be within our grasp.

***"Golf teaches me how to be my best."***

## June 11: Potential

We're the ones who dream. We're the ones who set the standards for what we want to accomplish. No one can create a dream for us. No one can tell us how good we should strive to be. It's up to us to decide what our potential is.

Understanding our potential is like trying to catch a feather on a windy day. That's because we don't know the things we don't know. What do we need to do to fulfill our potential? How much should we practice? Would lessons help? What exercise, diet, and sleep regimen would best suit us? Which tournaments should we play? Will we get better as we get older? How good can our golf swing be? What are we physically capable of doing? What are we mentally capable of doing? How should we develop our mental game to its fullest? How good can our short game be if we practice diligently? What should we read? Who can help us?

The question of whether we have reached our potential is a trick question. There's no concrete answer to it. We may feel we have tried everything to be our best. We may convince ourself that we have reached our potential. However, we never know what insight awaits us. We never know what chance meeting will provide some critical insight. We never know when we will learn exactly what has been missing that will tie everything together, leading to a breakthrough in performance.

As long as you have a desire to pursue your dreams, then you owe it to yourself to keep your dreams alive in some way. Dreams live in our spirit for a reason. They call us to keep moving forward. The destination may ultimately not be golfing greatness, but perhaps something even greater.

***"I live up to my standards and dreams."***

## June 12: Having Your Mind

The ability to manage our mind is developmental. It has some predictable characteristics and stages of development. Meditation trains our mind to quiet down and focus on one task, rather than jumping from topic to topic as if we were trying to watch many movies at one time.

For those who take the time and do the work involved in developing their capability to manage their mind, they will have a sense that they are in charge of what movies play in their mind. They will have a sense that they have a mind and can use it in ways that are most beneficial to them.

For those who have not developed their capability to manage their mind, they will have a sense that their mind has them and that it operates somewhat independently of their intentions. They will sometimes feel as if they are in a theater watching a movie and that there's someone in the control room changing movies at a whim.

***"I manage my thinking skillfully."***

## June 13: Playing Without Tension

Undue tension in life can cause health problems. Undue tension in golf creates poor decisions and poor swings. Tension, in both life and golf, is a choice we make, albeit a subconscious one for most of us. There are the exceptional individuals who choose to live or play golf with tension because it feels good to them to be on the edge, but most of us who play golf with tension don't consciously choose to have tension. To create tension for ourself, we unconsciously adopt beliefs about others and ourself that create both mental and physical tension in our life and golf game.

There are many beliefs that cause tension for people. However, there's one characteristic that all tension-causing beliefs have. The belief is that something is other than it should be. For example, we often hear golfers talk about the shots they shouldn't have hit, the putts they should have made, the bogeys that are utterly unacceptable, the scores for a round that are higher than they should be, and the lousy swings they shouldn't have made. All of these thoughts create tension in differing amounts in golfers who make the statements or think those thoughts.

The cure for tension is as uncomplicated as the understanding of the problem. Stop thinking that something should or shouldn't be happening. All of the wishing that something should or shouldn't have happened creates nothing other than tension. The alternative is to accept what happens as a fact. Whatever happens, happens. Accept that things happen that aren't our choice. That's part of life and golf.

A better approach is to take note of the things in our golf game that need development. In this case, we might hear a golfer say things such as, "I could use some practice to find a more consistent golf swing," "I'm going to work on my speed in putting," and "I'm going to work on course management so I can hit shots that are within my skill level." We recognize that there are areas of our golf game that we can improve, but we accept what happens and move forward.

***"I play golf freely."***

## June 14: Developing as a Golfer

Golf can be a perfect stage to develop ourself. As we develop in golf, we also develop in business, family, relationships, and life in general. Even though golf is a game, we usually play true to who we are as a person at the time. Who we are at our depths shapes our golf game and our life. Conversely, as we develop in life, we also can develop in our mental approach to golf.

Golf can teach us a lot about mental focus, managing our thinking and emotions, and learning to compete without reservation. We also learn about building confidence, removing self-imposed limits, learning to be more courageous, maintaining optimism even when we're in a slump, and learning to learn more effectively.

What do you need to develop in order to be a better golfer and person? What keeps you from being your best? What makes you unsure of yourself? What do you need to learn how to do?

***"I'm developing as a golfer and person."***

## June 15: More at Home

There's immense power in accepting who we are and what our golf game is. We can never feel at home in golf if we seek to be what others are. Ultimately, golf is a journey to discover who we are, experimenting with various approaches along the way, taking some paths that lead to dead ends, and finding other paths that work for us.

We discover things along the way about the ways we learn, about whether we play with finesse or power, whether we're conservative or aggressive, whether we love to compete or not, whether we prefer to be more social than not, and whether we truly believe in ourself or not. Whatever paths we choose, it's up to each of us to appreciate who we have chosen to become along the way. The journey is a success if we fell more at home than when we started.

***"I feel at home with my golf game."***

## June 16: More Motivated

Developing as a golfer means that we're clear, about both what we want and what we don't want. It's impossible to be highly motivated if we're unclear about what we truly want. We can't trust our motivation if it's constantly shifting. If we chase the latest fads, then we become a servant of the fads. Being highly motivated means we're clear about what we want, and our choices are consistent. That's not to say that course corrections are a mistake, but it is to say that constant course corrections make our motivations suspect in terms of providing lasting benefit.

***"I'm deeply motivated."***

## June 17: Changing and Growing

Development begets development. Often development is a series of small steps with nearly imperceptible levels of growth. Development is usually about changing and growing a little bit every day. We can wonder, on a daily basis, how much growth is happening. When we stay with our approach and have the broader understanding that comes with time, we can more easily see what's happened along the way.

Golf works that way. How much do we benefit from hitting a bucket of balls? How much do we benefit from practicing 100 putts? How much do we benefit from 100 chips? The changes in skill levels are imperceptible, but when we hit a bucket of balls every day for months and practice thousands of chips and putts, the evidence of growth becomes more obvious if we're practicing in the right ways. Imperceptible changes in development lead to perceptible changes in development.

***"I'm changing and growing."***

## June 18: Making Choices

As we develop, we become clearer about the life that we want. We also become more capable of making choices and doing the things we know we must do to have the life we want.

Golf teaches us the same thing. As we become more skilled and knowledgeable about golf, we become clearer about the golf game that we want. We also become clearer about the choices we need to make and the things that we must do to have the golf game that we want. We know that, without practice, we're going to remain in our present state. We know that if we continue to do what we've always done, we'll continue to get the results that we've always gotten.

We have to take steps forward to find the golf game that we want. What are the choices in golf that you need to make to move forward? What do you need to do next to move forward in golf?

***"I move forward in golf."***

## June 19: Letting Go as Development

For there to be growth in our golf game, we have to adopt new ways of thinking and new ways of behaving. That's the nature of development. Even if our new ways of thinking and behaving are only refinements of what they are currently, usually we have to let go of something before we can do something else. In golf, when we learn a new teacher's method, we have to let go of the method that preceded it.

Letting go is difficult for some of us. Most of us want to hold on to the familiar in some way. Beginning fresh for some of us feels like we are taking on too much risk. Fear gets in the way. We fear losing the comfort of the familiar, even if the familiar isn't great. Our thoughts can be, “What if I let go of what I have and the new situation turns out to be worse than what I already had?” Some of us are more risk averse than others. Change is more difficult for the risk averse, requiring more courage and energy to let go.

***“I let go of what stands in the way of my development.”***

## June 20: Present as Development

We know that it’s good to stay in the present when we play golf. We know that if we let our mind wander to past or future shots, putts, and scores, we can sabotage our round. We start to think and analyze too much. We know that we play best when we focus on the current shot or putt, giving ourself fully to the task at hand—not thinking too much, just playing golf.

The same thing is true with life in general. It’s good to stay in the present, staying connected to our senses, staying connected to how we’re feeling in the moment. It’s easy for our mind to wander, thinking of the past or future events because our mind tends to be highly active. Our mind wants something to do. Our mind will occupy itself with something if we don’t consciously manage our thinking and direct our attention to the present.

Staying in the present in life is a good thing to do for the same reasons that staying in the present in golf is. The present is worthy of our full attention. Even if there isn’t much going on at any one time, we find significant benefit by quieting our mind, attending to our senses, and appreciating the present for what it is.

***“I live in the present more.”***

## June 21: Our Identity

Conscious choices are an indication of development. We're becoming the author of our destiny. There are less unwanted habitual thought patterns, emotions, and behavioral patterns that feel out of our control. We can decide when and how we want to think about the past.

Thinking productively about the past is a useful task for learning about what to do in the present and future. When we learn to manage our thinking, we don't use memories of the past to define ourself narrowly or negatively. We can choose to define ourself in any way that seems useful and reasonable.

We can understand our past positively, even if there were difficult or troubling times. We can choose to learn from them, let them go, and define ourself by our positive experiences of the past. There isn't a universal law that says we must define ourself by our negative experiences of the past. That's a choice, usually a subconscious and unhelpful choice.

Golf teaches us the same lesson. We choose who we are as a golfer. We can remember our best shots or we can choose to remember our worst shots and mistakes. How we color ourself as a golfer is our choice. In addition, golf teaches us that clinging to the past is a formula for underperforming as a golfer. In golf, we let go of the past or future so that we can focus fully on the present.

***"I choose who I am as a golfer."***

## June 22: Thinking About the Future

When we become rooted in living in the present, it's easier to decide when it's appropriate to think about the future. When we have not fully embraced the present moment and our present self, our inclination will be to let our mind wander to the past or the future. We can also distract ourself from the present by doing pleasurable or stressful things.

Once we accept that we're not perfect but are good enough at this moment, it opens up the possibility of the present being a good place to be. It's easier to be present to others and ourself when we feel good about ourself. The present isn't an uncomfortable place to be.

When we feel good about the present, then we can be more objective about what the future might hold. If we're in pain in the present, the future is a place where we seek to relieve pain. The future doesn't look as expansive and full of possibility.

Golf teaches us the same lesson. When we can accept where we are at the present, that our game isn't perfect and that there are parts of our game that have some merit, then the future can be a place where we consider an expansive view of the possibilities of development. If we decide that our game is a total disaster, then we channel our thinking into narrow patterns of improvement, being like a firefighter and extinguishing the biggest flames. Healthy development is more about freely choosing who we want to be as a golfer and person.

***"I choose how I think about the future."***

## June 23: A Great Learner

Learning paves the way to discovery and growth. The more we learn, the more we can discover and know. The more we know, the more we can grow. Even if the knowledge that we gain is that something doesn't work, we have moved forward by eliminating something that may have been holding us back.

There are some characteristics that great learners have in common. They are willing to admit when they don't have all the answers. They don't fake it. Their willingness to admit they don't know something creates a search for knowledge in earnest.

Great learners are willing to step out of the commonplace and try new things. They realize that many experiments will yield unfruitful results, but they always gain some knowledge from the experiments.

Great learners are willing to seek help from others. No one has all the answers. Life is simply too complex to know everything required for success.

What do you not know right now that would be valuable to know? What experiments can you conduct to see how good you might become in golf? From whom might you need to seek help in moving forward in golf?

***"I'm a great learner."***

## June 24: Appreciating Our Growth

Appreciation is one of the greatest gifts we can give ourself. Appreciation opens us up to noticing the good things about life and us. It cleans the filters through which we see life. Often the only difference between being unhappy and happy is how we're viewing things.

Appreciating our growth adds momentum and motivation for more growth. It's a virtuous cycle. Growth begets growth. Motivation begets motivation. Momentum begets momentum.

In golf and the mental game in particular, growth happens when we can think in new ways, experience our emotions in new ways, and experience our senses and our bodies in new and empowering ways. Developing our mental game allows us to play golf more freely and spontaneously. We stop trying to micromanage the mechanical aspects of golf. We learn to trust our mind and body. We learn to be present and spontaneous as we play the game as opposed to playing with our swing mechanics during a round. We allow our mind to focus on hitting fantastic shots and putts and appreciating how good we're becoming. These things tell us that we're growing as a golfer.

***"I appreciate my growth."***

## June 25: Appreciating Others

Golf is a social endeavor. Even though we usually play golf as an individual sport, we always play in a group. Groups teach us about diversity and that others see things differently. Others respond with different emotions than we do. Others approach problems differently and have different strategies for getting things accomplished.

There are many ways to swing a golf club and many ways to manage our way around the golf course. Others teach us that. When we engage others in life and golf with an eye to discovering their ways of being, we can't help but understand them and ourself more richly than before. We create choices for ourself when we understand others and ourself better.

We can continue to do things our way, or we can choose to learn from others. We learn that others always have something to teach us if we will just look up and notice what's going on around us. Everyone has something to teach us, even if it's teaching us what sorts of things may not work for us.

***"I appreciate others around me."***

## June 26: Being Joyful

A sign that we're developing as a golfer is that we're able to rise above undesirable circumstances and be joyful. Being joyful is highly adaptive because it feels good to be joyful. It doesn't feel good to be angry, sad, or resentful. When we're able to rise above undesirable circumstances, we can say, "We have circumstances in our lives. Our circumstances don't have us."

Learning to be joyful, irrespective of circumstances, takes practice. With meditation, we learn how to cause a shift in our thinking, emotions, and physical states. We learn how to create our own internal circumstances.

Golf is the consummate teacher of how to rise above circumstances. Many circumstances in golf tend to be imperfect or even undesirable. Rarely, if ever, is everything just perfect, exactly how we would want it to be for the whole round of golf. We learn to accept and deal with "what is" in golf. Fighting with "what is" is a downward cycle of poor performance and excuse making. We learn that we perform the best when we can let go of all internal and external distractions, embrace the current shot and circumstances, and move forward with complete commitment. We learn that we're not a prisoner of our circumstances.

***"I'm joyful in the present moment."***

## June 27: Being Centered

The word "centered" is a metaphor for development. To center ourself means that we can easily move in any direction. From our center, we're never out of place, never preventing ourself from taking the desired course of action. From our center, we're always in balance, easily able to compensate for shifts in the environment around us.

In golf, when we center ourself, we're free to think, feel, and perform whatever is necessary to pursue our intentions. To center ourself is the opposite of feeling we're spinning out of control on the golf course. Even if we're not playing at our highest levels, there's a sense that everything is fine when we center ourself. Irrespective of what happens, we feel a sense of well-being and are glad to be where we are.

Complete the following sentences as spontaneously as possible with as many endings as possible. Record your answers for further reflection.

- In order to center my feelings on the golf course, I could...
- I could play golf from my center by...
- In order to center myself in life, I could...
- To center my thinking on the golf course, I'm going to...
- If I wanted to center myself socially, I would...
- The things that keep me from centering myself on the golf course are...
- The center myself more, I need to start...
- To center myself more, I need to stop...

Reflect on your answers, particularly the ones that seem the most emotionally significant. Imagine in the future being more the golfer and person you desire to be. Imagine feeling, thinking, and behaving more centered.

***"I play golf from my center."***

## June 28: Being Generous

When we feel wounded, insecure, and tentative in the world, the inclination for many of us is to be self-centered. We spend a lot of energy to meet our basic needs. We focus most of our energy on ourself. We can't care for others freely because we can't give away what we don't have. To give security to others, we must have security. To give true encouragement to others, we must know what it means to be encouraged. To give wisdom to others, we must have wisdom. As we become more developed, secure, and productive in the world, we can have more energy in our lives to care for others. We can become a deep well of positive energy for others.

The same principles apply in golf. As we become more secure in our game, have more knowledge and skill, and have more wisdom to manage our own mental game, we become more capable of reaching out to others when they need our help.

Some people seem to be naturally more generous than others. However, not everyone knows how to be supportive of others in ways that others can easily receive. For them, learning to be generous will require conscious effort, and trial and error.

***"I'm generous with those around me."***

## June 29: Strange Things

We live with all sorts of useful illusions. We live with the illusion that there are 24 hours in a day and 365 days per year, but every four years we have to add a day to the calendar to make things work out neatly. We also tend to think of gravity as being constant, but it isn't. As we increase in altitude, the force of gravity decreases. In fact, even the idea of altitude is a useful abstraction. We measure altitude relative to sea level, but the question is, "What sea?" The Dead Sea is 1300 feet below sea level.

Life is full of strange and amusing things if we will just open our mind to experience what's truly there rather than accepting abstractions as reality.

Golf is that way, too. There are many abstractions about what a good swing is, what a good putting stroke is, or what it means to play a good round of golf. However, what makes a good swing, a good putt, or a good round of golf depends on the perspective of the person thinking about them.

Learning to look for strange things in golf and life can open up pathways for learning. If we simply accept commonly held abstractions, we will fit in well but may not create anything new, interesting, and worthwhile.

***"I'm open to seeing things in new ways."***

## June 30: Your Dreams

We want to understand our subconscious mind because when we play in the zone, we are connecting with our subconscious mind. We rely on our subconscious mind to help create a strong mental game. We want to be comfortable with how our subconscious mind works and cooperate with it.

Our subconscious mind feels a bit dreamlike. That's why when a golfer is playing in the zone, it feels like a daydream. Golfers will even joke about the experience by saying, "Don't wake me up."

We need to be able to connect deeply with our subconscious mind. We can do that by learning to understand our dreams more clearly. Dreams are probably the least understood subconscious mental phenomena.

The key to understanding dreams is to take them as a symbol or metaphor. We usually don't take them literally. For example, suppose you have a dream of a mountain. Ask yourself, "What do I notice about the mountain?" You might have an answer such as, "It's a very steep and rugged mountain." Then ask, "Is there anything going on in my golf game that feels like a steep and rugged mountain?" "Should I be trying to climb the mountain?" "Do I need help to climb this mountain?" This line of questioning is how we can understand our dreams and subconscious mind. We approach them as symbols and metaphors.

***"I understand my dreams."***

# *July: Being in Training*

Great practice helps create great champions. Greatness begins on the range, the short-game area, and in your mind as you work on your mental game. The goal of great practice is to practice effectively and leave time to pursue other things in life along with golf.

## July 1: Practicing Mentally

The best practice simulates as much as possible the situations we find on the golf course while playing. When we think of practice, we need to think of both mental and physical practice.

Golfers understand the idea of physical practice. They go to the range and short-game area and hit shots and putts. They stretch and work out.

To practice mentally, you need to know the areas of your mental game that need development. Make a list of the areas of your mental game that need improvement. You might do this by remembering past rounds and competitions where you ran into difficulties. Once you've made a comprehensive list of the areas that need improvement, rank the list in order of what needs the most attention from you. That will give you a good starting list to help focus your efforts.

When you practice on the range, in the short-game area, or in practice rounds on the golf course, use your imagination to help you work on the areas of your mental game that need improvement. For example, suppose you get nervous over short putts. As you practice putting, imagine being in a competition feeling that same nervousness. What would you do to help calm your nerves? You might try different techniques such as deep breathing or progressive relaxation in which you consciously relax different muscles.

In this way, you're working on both your physical and mental games. You're working on your whole person, taking a holistic approach to improving your golf game.

***"I practice mentally and physically."***

## July 2: Focused Practice

Great focus creates great practice. We don't go to the range or short-game area without a game plan of what we need to practice and how. When our mind focuses on learning, which is the intent of any practice, our mind responds best when the focus is clear, and the skill to learn is small enough to grasp in the time allowed. If we have all day to practice, we may be able to focus on two or three things. If we have one hour, our focus is on one thing that's small in scope.

We focus on small things because our mind and body need clear feedback whether the practice is working. For example, if our focus is the whole putting stroke, we can't know what part of the putting stroke is working or not working. Is the problem with the grip, tempo, alignment, ball position, the backstroke, the forward stroke, feeling in the arms or shoulders, or width of stance? Do we have a problem with our mental game, and how we talk to ourself about our putting? Great practice needs clear focus and feedback.

***"I practice with a clear focus and feedback."***

## July 3: Dealing With Pressure

Common wisdom says that the best way to become good at dealing with pressure is to gain experience in pressure situations. Compete and put ourself in pressure situations, and we will get better. There's some merit to the approach, but it doesn't always work. Repetition doesn't necessarily equate to improvement, unless we do some things differently. There are other approaches to dealing with pressure.

Another approach is to let go of our obsessions with results. We want to pay attention to our results, but not be obsessed with them. By focusing obsessively on results, we're placing undue emphasis on any one event or outcome. It can start to feel like a life or death event, which it isn't. It's a competition, a tournament, or a round.

Another way of dealing with pressure is to rehearse, imaginatively, yourself playing in situations that would normally cause you to feel under pressure. Imagine feeling calm and relaxed, enjoying being in the situation.

When you practice physically, imagine you're playing in situations that have the outcome of the match or tournament attached to it. Imagine you're making perfect swings, feeling confident, enjoying the situation, being mentally strong, and rising to the occasion.

Another way of dealing with pressure is to practice being present to your task. Being present is focusing on the swing or putting stroke you're making, not focusing on the outcome of the swing. Being present is about learning to discipline your mind to focus on the activity that you're doing and leaving the results to be what they are.

***"I deal with pressure well."***

## July 4: ABCs of Target Golf

Pressure tends to cloud our thinking and limit choices in shot selection. One of the biggest mistakes players make is to choose, automatically, an aggressive target after a bad shot or a bad hole, as if they are trying to make up for the bad shot or hole. The best antidote for this kind of thinking is always to consider multiple possible targets. Thinking of a number of possible targets is a good habit to develop. The habit begins in practice, either on the range or in a practice round.

Think of every shot as having three possible targets: an "A" target, a "B" target, and a "C" target. An "A" target is the ideal, perfect outcome but is the highest risk shot. A "B" target is an excellent outcome and is less risky. A "C" target is a good outcome and is a low-risk shot.

The rule of thumb is to hit only shots that you have at least a 90% chance of accomplishing. If we can't hit the "A" target 90% of the time, then we choose the "B" target. If we can't hit the "B" target 90% of the time, then we choose the "C" target. The idea is two-fold—always consider multiple targets and always choose a high-probability shot.

The ideal place to begin practicing this approach is in practice rounds on the golf course, which allow you to experiment with different targets and see if you can pull off the shots you think you have a high probability of success, even if they are aggressive targets.

***"I choose my targets wisely."***

## July 5: Mechanical Swing Thoughts

A mechanical swing thought describes what our body is doing abstractly. For example, a golfer might say to himself, "I'm taking the club more inside as I begin my downswing." The phrase is abstract because it doesn't tell us how far inside the swing is going, nor does it tell us what the "beginning the downswing" means. Is the beginning of the downswing the first inch or the first foot or something else? That's the nature of mechanical swing thoughts. They are abstract descriptions of what we're trying to do concretely.

Mechanical swing thoughts are fine for learning new movements because we want to simplify things as much as possible and avoid burying ourself in detail. Too much detail while trying to learn something new is counterproductive.

The problem with mechanical swing thoughts begins when players take the mechanical swing thoughts from the range to the golf course to play a round of golf. Mechanical swing thoughts might work well for a round or two, but players eventually find that, at some point, they no longer work well. The experience would be similar to trying to drive a car with a map entirely covering the windshield. The driver may know the destination and have some of the right tools but is using the tools incorrectly. Mechanical swing thoughts are for the range only and are only for learning new moves.

***"I use mechanical swing thoughts for learning."***

## July 6: Swing Feelings

Swing feelings are more specific and powerful than mechanical swing thoughts. That's so because the feeling of any bodily sensation is unique and personal. For example, suppose that you and I are both trying to make a "full shoulder turn" as part of our golf swing. The feelings that we have in our bodies as we make that movement are unique. Because we have differently shaped bodies and different degrees of flexibility and are different ages, our bodily movements will be different and feel differently to us.

In addition, a swing feeling is more easily verified than a mechanical swing thought. With a mechanical swing thought, we would need video or a third party to verify that we're doing what we intended to do. With a swing feeling, we know whether we felt what we wanted during the swing. We don't need anything else to verify that. We either felt it, or we didn't.

Having swing feelings allows us to know our swing more intimately and to own it. Our physical sensations are intensely intimate and personal.

If you're not in the habit of paying attention to bodily movements, it will take some time for you to develop awareness of subtle bodily movements. Be patient with yourself if you don't have the ability immediately. For most, it takes time to develop a subtle awareness.

Swing feelings are good for practice on the range and play on the golf course. Swing feelings engage the right part of the brain that plays and performs, rather than analyzing our body mechanics as we try to play.

***"I use effective swing feelings."***

## July 7: Target Swing Thoughts

The goal is to learn to "play automatically" as the great ball striker, Moe Norman said. To play automatically is to have ingrained the movements in our golf swing, so that our swing is an unconscious movement. We can do that only if we know what our swing is and have stuck with it long enough to learn it to the point of unconsciousness.

The reason playing automatically makes sense is that athletic movements are fast and complicated, faster and more complicated than the conscious mind can handle at full speed. To play mechanically is to limit what our mind and body do athletically.

If we liberate our conscious mind from focusing on the mechanics of the swing, what should its focus be? Our mind needs to focus on something. Having a blank mind is impossible. Even when we sleep, our mind is active.

The answer is to fill your mind with targets for every shot and putt. Hold a picture of your target in your mind before, during, and after a swing or putting stroke.

Using targets as a swing thought works on the range and the golf course during play. When you're warming up or practicing on the range, you can use a combination of mechanical, feel, and target swing thoughts. This routine is a good warm-up for your mind as well and gets you tuned into what you want to do with your swing. However, when you go to the course to play, let the mechanical thoughts stay on the range.

***"I focus on targets during my swing."***

## July 8: Tempo Swing Thoughts

Tempo swing thoughts are a type of feel swing thought. Tempo swing thoughts are good because they focus on what our body is doing in a concrete manner, unlike a mechanical swing thought. Tempo swing thoughts keep our swing or putting stroke on a tempo suited to us as individuals. Players vary greatly with what feels like a good tempo to them. That's true of players at all levels. We have to find a tempo that feels natural and that we can repeat. That's the key to a consistent golf swing.

A great way of feeling the tempo of a swing or putting stroke is to use the words "tick" and "tock." Begin your swing or stroke with the word "tick" and use the word "tock" at impact with the ball. Don't think about the words themselves so much, but hear the "sound" of the word in your head as you say it to yourself.

In addition, when you're practicing on the range or short-game area, and say the words "tick" and "tock," notice the physical feelings you have in your body when your body moves at the tempo that you're practicing. Learn to recognize the feeling of a good tempo swing or putting stroke.

When you go to the course to play, you can continue to use the tempo swing thought as long as you're still able to feel yourself swinging or putting to a target.

***"I play with great tempo."***

## July 9: A Game Plan

To fail to plan is to plan to fail. Even if you have a vision of how you want things to go for you, that's not enough. Even if you have a vision and goals, they aren't enough. Visions and goals tell you what you want to accomplish. A plan tells you how you're going to accomplish your vision and goals. One without the other is incomplete.

Your confidence in a plan grows as it becomes more specific and more detailed about how you'll achieve what you want. Don't worry if you don't feel like you have all the data that you need to make a perfect plan. Any plan makes assumptions. We can't know everything. Begin today to create a one-year plan and a three-year plan. What do you need to do to become the player you dream of being?

***"I trust and follow my plan."***

## July 10: Structured Practices

When you practice, do things in groups or sets, similar to how athletes work out with weights. For example, if you're working on 30-yard pitch shots, hit 10 pitches in a set with the goal of having them end up within eight feet of the hole. After you hit the 10 pitches, go up to the hole and see how many pitches are within eight feet. For the next set, see if you can beat your previous total with the next set of 10 pitches.

Decide in advance how many sets you might like to practice. A large bucket of balls is about 100 balls. You might set out to practice 10 sets of 10 balls. This approach helps give structure to your practice. It also builds in feedback, so that you know if you're improving with each set. Unstructured practice can be unproductive. In addition, having a long practice session isn't a good substitute for a short, focused, structured practice with clear feedback.

***"I practice in a focused and structured way."***

## July 11: Important Statistics

Statistics are helpful to decide what we need to improve in our game. They are objective, so it's hard to rationalize our way into thinking we're good at some parts of our game when the numbers don't support our belief. However, unless you're a Tour player with easily available statistics, you'll want to manage what statistics you gather. Here are three key stats that you can easily track.

### *Greens in Regulation*

Greens in regulation (GIR) tell us the quality of our ball striking. It tells us directly about our ability to hit fairway metals, hybrids, irons, and wedges to greens. PGA Tour leaders are typically about 75% GIR. The reason this is a good statistic is that it relates closely to getting the ball in the hole and making a good score. This is the "meat and potatoes" of scoring. If we have a high percentage of GIR, we have many opportunities to make pars and birdies. A combination of high GIR along with being a good putter is a powerful combination.

### *Putts per GIR*

Putts per GIR are an uncluttered indicator of the quality of our putting. It gets to the heart of the matter. Can we putt well when we have a chance to make birdie or eagle? Can we two-putt greens when we don't hit the ball close to the hole? PGA Tour leaders will be about 1.73 putts per GIR at season's end. They make many putts once they get the ball on the green.

*Scrambling*

The third statistic is scrambling, which is the percentage of time a golfer gets up and down when she has missed the green in regulation. This is a great statistic because it directly measures our ability to save rounds and post a good score. Even the best on the PGA Tour will miss 25% of greens in regulation. That means that they will miss between 4-5 greens in regulation, potentially meaning the difference between 4-5 shots or more per round. In addition, the statistic is a good one because it measures the whole short game, both pitching, chipping, and putting. The PGA Tour leaders in this category will scramble successfully about 65% of the time by season's end.

What are your goals for GIR, Putts per GIR, and Scrambling?

***"I track the progress of my game."***

## July 12: Pre-Shot Routines

Pre-shot routines serve vital purposes, which are making good decisions about strategy, getting ourself ready to hit a shot or putt, and keeping our analytical mind as quiet as possible.

Good pre-shot routines don't overuse our analytical ability. We want to get the essential information, make good decisions, and keep the process as simple as possible. We want to use our imagination more than we use our analytical ability during our pre-shot routine.

Once you've made a decision about the target, club, and swing to use, commit to what you've decided, and hit the shot. Forget about the "what if" analysis once you've decided on a target, club, and swing. It's counterproductive at that point.

Some people feel that they can never have enough data to make perfect decisions. They then become paralyzed by the process, activating the analytical part of their mind until it's highly active. For these golfers, the challenge is to learn to let go a bit and trust themselves. Deep down it's a matter of self-trust and reliance. Choose to believe in yourself.

***"I have a simple and effective pre-shot routine."***

## July 13: Coaches

We can get the most out of a lesson with either a swing coach or mental game coach by understanding what part of our brain we are using. Swing coaches work mostly with the left side of the brain, teaching swing concepts and mechanics. Mental coaches work mostly with the right side of the brain, teaching clients how to use their brains in the most effective way while playing and practicing.

We need both sides of our brain, but we have to learn when and how to engage the correct part of the brain for the correct activity. The left brain is most helpful when we're learning a new skill. We want to be conscious of what we're doing. We want to analyze, understand, and study a new skill until it becomes a habit. We want to be conscious of swing mechanics while we're learning, experimenting, or refining our golf game on the range or in the short-game area.

We want to engage the right brain when we're playing golf or working on our mental game. We can't play in the zone if we're fussing with mechanics on the golf course. It's a guaranteed approach to be "zone free" for the round. To play using the right brain, focus on what you are feeling and hitting your ball to targets. Keep things simple—feeling the swing you want as opposed to using mechanical swing thoughts. Stay loose between shots by thinking of things other than golf.

***"I get the most from coaches."***

## July 14: Imagine, Feel, Target

There are three parts to this pre-shot routine, "imagine," "feel," and "target."

In the "imagine" part of the pre-shot routine, imagine you're making the swing that you want. Don't move your body. Just use your imagination to either picture the swing or imagine what it would feel like to make your swing.

During the "feel" part of the pre-shot routine, take your practice swing and try to duplicate what you imagined. Feel the same movement in your body that you imagined.

During the "target" part of the pre-shot routine, take another practice swing holding only your target in your mind, thereby trusting your swing and just allowing yourself to swing automatically to the target that you have in your mind.

Then you're ready to step up and hit your shot.

***"I imagine, feel, and swing to my target."***

## July 15: Imagining Feel

In the same way that we can practice imaginatively, we can imagine how things feel as we practice. This is a good habit to develop because the more we know how our swing feels, the faster our swing can become a habit and then become unconscious. The more our swing becomes unconscious, the more we own our swing and can focus on playing golf, rather than playing golf swing.

To imagine the feel of your swing, imagine you're taking a swing in slow motion. Imagine your body moving inch by inch, very slowly. Imaginatively, notice what part of your body you feel when you imagine making a swing. What sensations would you feel? What would you feel in your legs, feet, back, shoulders, arms, hands, fingers, neck, and even your facial muscles? Now imagine you're hitting shots from different lies and how that might feel.

***"I imagine how it feels to play great golf."***

## July 16: One-Off Swing Thoughts

When we describe something as being "one-off," it means that it isn't exactly what we want. A one-off swing thought is mechanical in nature. We're thinking about particular physical movements, which are part of our golf swing. For example, a common mechanical swing thought would be to think about making a "full shoulder turn." This is both a mechanical and a one-off swing thought. It's a one-off swing thought because golfers use the swing thought in hopes of accomplishing something else in their golf swing. For example, someone may use the "full shoulder turn" swing thought in order to hit the ball with more power. Our true intent is to hit the ball with more power. There are many ways to accomplish that. A "full shoulder turn" is only one way of doing that.

One-off swing thoughts are fine, often producing results for a time, but they eventually stop working and become unhelpful. They do this because the nature of the golf swing is a complex system of bodily movements and sequences. By using a one-off swing thought, we're focusing only on a small part of the golf swing. We're not allowing the power of our subconscious mind to assist us in getting the results that we truly want. Our subconscious mind is a clever bit of technology that's available to us. We let it work for us when we use swing thoughts that are more about the result that we want, rather than focusing on how to get the result.

One-off swing thoughts try to control our movements by consciously telling our body how to do its job. The strategy doesn't work very well athletically. When we tie our shoes, we don't consciously tell our fingers, hands, and arms how to move. We just let go and let them give us our desired result. It's like magic. They just know what to do. Why should golf be any different? When you practice, hold your intention clearly in mind, while allowing your body to give you the results you intend.

***"I hold my intention in mind."***

## July 17: Practicing to Improve

There's a difference between practicing for improvement versus practicing for enjoyment. Both are acceptable, but we should be clear about our intentions. Some people love to hit golf balls or practice their short game. It's a good, healthy way to entertain ourselves. However, practicing for entertainment is highly unlikely to produce significant improvements in our game. At best, we're reinforcing what's already somewhat habitual and perhaps maintaining some degree of fitness. Intentional practice, on the other hand, sets out consciously to be able to do or to learn something that's new, non-habitual, or unknown.

Ask yourself, "What is it that I want to do or know today that will help me be a better player?" If the answer is "nothing," then practicing for enjoyment is an excellent activity. If something comes to mind, then you should be practicing with intention, creating a plan for how you'll practice.

***"I practice intentionally."***

## July 18: Warm-Up Affirmations

When warming up on the range, we want to warm up our mind and our body. Meditation is a wonderful way to warm up your mind. Further, the affirmations in this book are a terrific source of affirmations to use while warming up.

For example, if you're working on ball striking, you can go to the ball striking chapter of this book, review the affirmations, and find ones that are appropriate for you to use on the range to warm up. To use an affirmation on the range, do the following. Before you hit a shot or putt, take a deep breath and mindfully repeat an affirmation to yourself. Then hit your shot or putt.

***"I warm up my mind with affirmations."***

## July 19: Your Wonderful Swing

Many golf swings get the job done. Some produce power, others accuracy, and others the ability to shape shots.

In contrast, there's only one version of you with your shape, size, and athletic ability. Your body functions to play golf in its own way. Some bodies lend themselves to power, some to accuracy, and others to athleticism with high degrees of hand-eye coordination.

Find what works best for you, call that your wonderful swing, and stay with it. Perfect it. Enjoy coming to the golf course with the same swing every time. Stay with the same swing as long as you can, until your body changes over time. As you age and your body changes, you may need to change your swing, unless you're fortunate and can have a swing that lasts a lifetime.

What's your swing optimized to do? What's your body optimized to do?

***"I know how my wonderful swing looks and feels."***

## July 20: The Feel of Golf

Some players are more naturally "feel players" than others. When golfers play with feel, it means that they pay more attention to the feelings in their body as they play as opposed to paying attention to mechanics of the swing and putting stroke. Playing by feel is an intuitive and imaginative way to play as opposed to being analytical and mechanical during a round.

Golfers are naturally inclined to play more as either a feel player or a mechanical player. Both approaches are useful and have their strengths and weaknesses.

However, everyone must become a feel player to some degree because of the nature of how our mind works. The mechanical approach to golf engages the analytical part of the mind, which is perfect when a player is in a learning mode. However, when we're playing on the golf course, we want to be in playing mode and not learning mode. Being in playing mode happens when we're more imaginative and intuitive about playing. In the playing mode, we activate the imaginative and intuitive parts of our mind, which helps us play in the zone.

Start paying attention to how your body feels as you play golf and practice on the range and in the short-game area. You can learn to listen to what your body is telling you. If you're more mechanical by nature, it will seem difficult as first, but everyone can learn to pay more attention to what their body is telling them.

***"I play golf with feel."***

## July 21: Golf as Development

When you're working on a part of your game, you should see it in terms of a development process. Development is a systematic process with incremental improvements. The best way to do this is to work backwards in your planning. Envision the desired result. Then plan backwards and see if you can identify the steps along the way that it would take to get you to your desired destination. It's like planning a trip. Understand where you want to go first, and then work your way backwards to where you are.

What do you need to work on in golf? What's the end goal? What are the steps along the way to get there?

***"I plan my development."***

## July 22: Playing Pebble

Let's suppose that you've never played Pebble Beach Golf Links before, and you're going to play there in the near future. You're looking forward to it. You've seen how beautiful it is on TV. You imagine how it will be when you play. You imagine that everything is going to be great. You'll be happy to be there. The weather is going to be perfect. You'll play great and enjoy the experience completely. It's a trip and experience of a lifetime.

Whether you're aware of it or not, when you used your imagination to picture yourself playing at Pebble, you were practicing mentally. You were preparing mentally to play. It's a good practice to imagine that you feel ready, and conditions are perfect, but what if it turns out that when you play, the weather is foggy, cold, and there are 20-25 mph winds? With your current mental practice, you only prepared to play in perfect conditions.

The lesson here is that we sometimes play golf in challenging conditions. Mental practice is about preparing to play well in good conditions and adverse conditions. When conditions are adverse, it's unhelpful to complain about them or wish they weren't adverse. They are what they are, and if we accept that, we will likely play much better and enjoy our round more than if we wished the conditions were better.

When you practice, imagine playing various courses and holes. Imagine different conditions and different situations in a tournament. Imagine you're enjoying adverse conditions because you're so strong mentally. Imagine that you have a competitive edge because you've prepared for whatever comes. Rehearse how you want to feel, how you want to act, how you want to look, and how you want to carry yourself. Imagine you're the superb competitor that you know you are deep inside.

***"I use my imagination to learn to play in all conditions."***

## July 23: Slow-Speed Practice

The full-speed swing is a blur and a barrage of sensations that are too numerous to appreciate consciously. Therefore, there are powerful lessons we can learn by practicing in slow speed. The key to success with slow-speed practice is to notice the subtle feelings that occur as we make swings, pitches, chips, and putting strokes.

In addition to understanding what we feel as we practice, we can pick up faults in mechanics that we might otherwise miss because we're so naturally athletic, that our bodies can make incredible compensations for us.

***"I understand my golf game at slow speed."***

## July 24: High-Speed Practice

Practicing at higher speeds than normal is a useful activity. It is particularly useful for players who tend to be analytical in nature. Analytical players require more time to gather data and make decisions. Practicing at a higher than normal speed helps us play with more feel and intuition. There simply isn't enough time to do the usual analysis prior to a shot.

Try playing a round of golf by yourself early in the morning or late in the evening when you're more likely to be undisturbed by other players. Play as fast as you can without paying conscious attention to yardages. Just pull clubs that look about right. Hit shots without much thought. Make putts without much green reading—just quickly notice the slopes, and let it go. Just let go and play with intuition and feel. Trust your intuition and feel. Notice how good it feels to play with imagination.

***"I practice at high speed."***

## July 25: Target Practice

Our goal is to be able to play and putt to targets only, without any thoughts of mechanics. That gives us the best chances of playing in the zone on a more regular basis. If that's the goal, then playing to targets has to be a regular part of our practice.

To do that, have practice sessions where you forget about mechanics totally, and you focus only on targets. Even if you're in the process of changing your swing, it's crucial to keep playing to targets. In addition, as you play to targets, you'll receive excellent feedback. You'll know how much the changes you're making have become habitual and unconscious.

To swing and putt to targets, you hold an image of the target in your mind before, during, and after every shot and putt. If there's any other thought other than the image of the target, then you've not yet fully played to targets. Playing to targets is like being in an IMAX theater where the only focus of your attention is what you see in front of you.

***"I play golf to targets."***

## July 26: Finding New Confidence

Find a place in your sanctuary where you're deeply confident. You may go to a new place in your sanctuary that you haven't visited before now. You may even have to take a journey in your sanctuary to a time and place where you find yourself deeply confident. When you're there, notice how you feel. In what part of your body do you feel deeply confident? Many people feel it in their chest, others in their gut. Some feel freedom in their movements. Others feel a confident gait as they walk. Where do you feel deeply confident? If deep confidence had a color associated with it, what color would it be?

Imagine practicing and playing with the same confident feelings in your body. Imagine wearing clothes with the color that signifies confidence to you. Imagine and feel how good it is to practice and play golf with deep, new confidence. Keep returning to this place in your sanctuary as you build the habit of deep confidence in your golf game.

***"I find deep levels of confidence in my golf game."***

## July 27: Owning Your Swing

The secret to owning our golf swing is to choose a swing that fits us and then stick with it. Some golfers become addicted to endless tweaking of their golf swing, believing that when they finally find the perfect mechanics for their swing, magically, they will be the champion they dream of being. We need only to look at the top Tour players to realize that there are many ways to swing a golf club effectively. There's no such thing as one perfect swing. There are many great swings.

The second secret to owning your golf swing is to know the key positions that you want to have in your golf swing. You also want to recognize the feelings that you have in your body as your body moves to those positions. After enough repetition, the feelings become familiar, far more familiar than an abstract swing thought could ever be. See if you can identify 3-5 key positions in your golf swing, along with the feelings that you have in your body when you make a good swing.

The third secret to owning your golf swing is to begin to trust your swing by practicing swinging to targets without thoughts of mechanics on the range and then on the course. Eventually, you want your swing to be unconscious, to where you can simply focus on targets and let your mind and body do what they need to do. You should begin trusting your swing at some point. Why not start today?

***"I own my swing."***

## July 28: Practicing in Your Imagination

We can do a lot of practicing without ever going to the golf course. We can practice mentally in a matter of minutes versus going to the range or short-game area.

All you need to do to practice mentally is to imagine making swings, hitting shots, and playing tournaments. Imagine playing in the near and distant future, playing all sorts of golf courses in all sorts of conditions. Imagine playing difficult golf courses and hitting shots and putts that are challenging. Imagine playing beautifully, enjoying golf more than ever before.

Mental practice is powerful because our subconscious mind doesn't make a distinction between what we do and what we imagine. They are both real to our subconscious mind. Think about your dreams. They feel real when we experience them, and they can affect us powerfully. Dreams and imagination are the languages of our subconscious mind.

***"I use my imagination to practice."***

## July 29: Range Practice

This is a practice routine to get maximum repetitions on the range without pounding a large number of golf balls. Get a small bucket of balls, which is about 30 balls. First, pick out a target. Even on the range, always have a target. Then, close your eyes or look down at the ground and imagine you're making the great swing you'll need to hit the ball to the target you chose. Do this imagining part without moving your body. Next, take a practice swing, feeling the same swing that you imagined yourself making. Then, take another practice swing with only your target in mind, trusting your mind and body to create the right swing. Then step up to the ball and hit it while you hold only your target in mind. Just let your body make the swing that you felt in your practice swing. Your body will know what it needs to do.

If you do this process for each of the 30 balls, it should take you about 30 minutes to hit a small bucket. What you'll find is that you get a clear sense of the swing you're trying to groove. It's crystal clear. You may also feel that your mind wants a bit of rest after you finish. Remember that you're developing new "muscles" in your mind. This practice is a bit like working new muscles in the gym. After a while, you'll develop more stamina and capability.

The reasons why this method works so well are that you're both maximizing the value of the repetitions, and you're giving your mind a clear picture of what you want it and your body to do for you. In addition, you're maximizing the value of the right kinds of repetitions. Repetitions are great, but they have to be the right repetitions for your mind to get a clear picture. When you imagine yourself making a swing, you're communicating effectively with your mind and telling it exactly what you want. You're giving it your vision of a wonderful golf swing.

By using this method, you'll experience a quiet mind. It's a way of engaging the imaginative part of your mind and quieting the analytical part of your mind. It's a way of practicing mindfulness, which is about paying close attention to your present experience. If you hit 30 balls this way, you'll have a good physical and mental workout with your mind and body in sync. You'll have built some solid brain circuitry on your way to a grooved swing.

***"I practice mindfully."***

## July 30: Complete Focus

Mindfulness is a way of being fully present to what we're doing. Think of the last couple of rounds you played. How present were you on the golf course? Did you totally focus on golf or was your mind wandering to other things? Most people allow some distractions into their golf game. Increasingly, some golfers take their phones to the golf course, ensuring that they will be distracted. Learning to let go of life for a while and just focusing on golf can take some practice and discipline.

Try practicing and playing with complete focus and awareness with every shot and every putt. Treat every shot and putt as if it were the last one. That's what it means to give your full attention to a shot or putt.

Complete focus is a powerful ability to possess. We can choose to block out everything that might be a distraction, having our mind focus fully on the current task, which is only to hit the next shot or putt. We can't play in the zone when our mind is wandering to things that weigh on our consciousness. To play in the zone is to give our full attention to what we're doing as if we're in a dream that has our full attention.

***"I practice and play with complete focus."***

## July 31: Being Optimistic in Practice

Golf can be difficult and sometimes frustrating because it can take a lot of time and effort before we see progress. It takes patience and persistence to stay at the task of learning something when progress seems slow in coming. Our attitude about what we're doing can either help us or hinder us. If we're impatient and angry with ourself because progress is slow, we're only adding to the difficulty of the task. If we're patient and encouraging of ourself, we create a friendly learning environment.

We must believe deeply that even if something takes us a long time to figure out that the journey will be worth it. Believe in yourself. Never let yourself say or believe that you won't get it. You'll get it. You can figure out anything in time.

***"I'm always optimistic in practice."***

# *August: Being A Free Spirit*

We can treat golf as a way to develop ourself mentally, emotionally, physically, and spiritually. To be on the path of spiritual development is to become freer to pursue our dreams, be our best, and be a gift to the world.

## August 1: Free Spirit

Being a free spirit means that we're free to grow, evolve, change, and become who we want to be. Being a free spirit means that we can reasonably expect to experience more breakthroughs in golf and life than those who have not tapped fully into the power of their spirit and their sanctuary.

From your sanctuary, imagine you're free to change, grow, and experience breakthroughs. Imagine that you're freely managing your thinking, emotions, and physical states. Imagine that you live your dreams. Imagine that you're using all of your athletic ability. Imagine whatever has been holding you back disappears. Imagine how good it is to be a free spirit.

***"I'm a free spirit."***

## August 2: The Art of Detachment

There's an instinctive desire that we have to attach ourselves to people, things, and ideas. We learn that from our earliest stages of development. Babies attach themselves to their mothers, fathers, and their family. Forming attachments is healthy. However, remaining attached and dependent as we mature isn't healthy. Part of maturity is learning detachment so that new relationships and ideas about life can take hold.

Detachment is also part of golf. As we take up the game, we attach ourselves to approaches for playing golf. As we gain experience in golf and mature in our game, we no longer remain dependent on some approaches, people, and relationships. We naturally begin to depend more on our own experience and judgment. It doesn't mean that we change everything about our golf game. It does mean that some things will naturally change as we become clear about our approach to playing golf.

***"I play golf freely."***

## August 3: Freedom to Grow

Our spirit naturally wants the freedom to explore, grow, learn, and change. The only reason it doesn't naturally do that is when we stifle it. Some of us fear freedom because it makes us responsible for creating the life we want and making our dreams come true.

In the short run, it can seem an easier choice to blame others, our background, our education, or our lack of opportunities for not being and doing what our dreams call us to fulfill. In the end, our spirit suffers like a bird in a small cage when we don't accept responsibility, risk failure, and go for what we truly desire.

***"My spirit expands, grows and explores."***

## August 4: Playing Golf Blissfully

Anthony de Mello, a Jesuit priest and spiritual mentor, taught that the only thing that keeps us from bliss at any moment is that we're thinking about what we don't have. The phenomenon that creates unhappiness or any other emotional state other than bliss is a focus on what's missing.

If we think about it and the connection with golf, the idea also applies. If we're unhappy about shooting 80, then we're focusing on the fact that we didn't shoot 79 or better.

A healthier way to play golf or live life is to focus on being thankful for what we have. For example, if we make a bogey and that normally makes us unhappy, rather than focusing on the fact that we didn't make par, we focus on how thankful we are to be playing golf or focus on how thankful we are to have more holes to play to make pars and birdies. Create the habit of always being thankful for something in your golf game, rather than focusing on what's missing.

***"I play golf blissfully."***

## August 5: A Quiet Spirit

Our spirit is in touch with our deepest wisdom. Our spirit is like having a person of consummate wisdom living within us. Sometimes our spirit hungers for more in life. Sometimes our spirit seeks to play. Sometimes our spirit simply seeks to be quiet and recharge. There's wisdom that our spirit wants to share with us when we need it.

Life sometimes feels as if it's at high speed. Technology has greatly aided our ability to do many things that were inconceivable only a few years ago. Technology and speed are good things. However, most of us don't thrive when we try to live at high speed all the time. Our bodies, minds, emotions, and spirits become weary and need rest.

Golf can be a perfect game to calm us and get us in touch with our quiet spirit. Golf can be relaxing if we just let go and enjoy playing, being in nature, and being with others doing the same. We can still compete while playing quietly, but there's a different feel to the round and a different feel to the competition. The urgency and importance of any one shot fades a bit. There's a bit of distance from the emotional impact that the game would ordinarily have. Try playing with a quiet spirit.

***"I play with a quiet spirit."***

## August 6: The Spirit's Perspective

When we meditate, we connect with our spirit's perspective. When we're quiet and in touch with our spirit, there's a timeless quality to the experience. When meditating deeply, it's difficult to know how long we have been meditating. A minute can seem like an hour and hours like minutes. Our spirit seems to step out of time as we experience it in our daily, busy lives. Our spirit takes the broad and long view of things. There's no rush to do or be anything. Things have a natural rhythm and timing that often don't meet with our modern pace of change.

In golf, we can experience our spirit's rhythm when we play in the zone. When we play in the zone, we're in touch with our spirit. We lose track of time. We immerse ourself in the moment. Things are easy and have a natural flow to them. When the round is over, it may seem as if it went by quickly or slowly. All we know for sure is that it was a wonderful experience.

***"I feel the natural flow and rhythm of my spirit."***

## August 7: Being the Best

Our spirit appreciates excellence. Our spirit wants to see what we can accomplish, and to stretch our understanding of who we can be in golf and life.

People have varying abilities of athleticism and aptitude for golf. Not everyone has the innate ability to be a touring professional. That's the nature of being human. Some people pick up the game quickly while most take time. Some people take up the game early, while others take up the game later in life. Golf is a great game that we can play for a lifetime if we stay healthy. Golf allows us to see how good we can become, even as our bodies change over the years. With golf, there's never a sense of finally mastering the game because we can always improve.

***"I'm discovering how good I can be."***

## August 8: Positive Spirit

Golf is a hard game. Everyone, even at the highest levels, makes mistakes on the golf course. We're always falling short of perfection. That's the nature of golf, always trying for perfection but always falling short. For that reason, golf invites us to be extreme optimists. Without that, we could become an angry, disappointed golfer.

When we're in touch with our spirit, we find extreme optimism. Our spirit knows no boundaries, no limitations, and no sense of failure. Even in the gloomiest of times, our spirit wants to bounce back and believe, hope, learn, and grow.

***"I'm always positive."***

## August 9: Meaning of Things

For some of us, the scores we shoot or how we play determines how we feel. If we have a good round, we're happy. If we have a poor round, we're sad. The very same score can make one player happy and another sad. One player who shoots 75 might feel ecstatic. Another player who shoots 75 might feel seriously disappointed.

With either case, when a score determines how we feel about a round, then we're giving over the power of our feeling to golf. Rather than playing golf, golf is playing us. We become a victim of golf.

One of the great joys of maturing is that we can decide what things mean. We can decide what scores mean. If we have a high scoring round by our standards, we can decide what it means to us. Rather than understanding the round as something bad, a sign of failure, or as a disappointment, we can give it some other meaning. We can understand it as one round where we weren't our best. We can understand it as a learning experience. There are many ways of understanding what a round of golf means. When we live and play from our spirit, we decide what things mean. We live and play more in tune with our true Self.

***"I decide what golf means."***

## August 10: Our Shadow Side

Carl Jung, the Swiss psychologist, talked about the concept of the "shadow." The shadow is the part of our personality that we would prefer to ignore. Further, our shadow may be unknown to us at a conscious level.

We become aware of our shadow when we see it in others. For example, suppose there's someone who we dislike or would rather avoid. That person may be awakening our shadow.

When we see behavior in others that we dislike, the question we should ask ourself is, "Is there something about that person's behavior that's relevant to how I behave or have behaved in the past?" We may find that we're more alike the person whom we disapprove of than we would like to be. That's becoming aware of our shadow side.

The awareness of our shadow provides the opportunity for spiritual growth. Golf can be a wonderful laboratory for learning about ourself and developing as a person and golfer. Golf is a competitive and social game, where people reveal sides of themselves that they hide in other settings, such as work or home. Once we recognize our shadow, we can choose to be different and act differently, or we can become more accepting of who we are. When we're blind to our own shadow, we have no choice to act differently.

More self-awareness brings more choices of who we choose to be and what we apply our energy to in life and golf. We're freer to give more of our energy to things we care about and truly desire rather than what we're subconsciously trying to avoid.

***"I'm self-aware."***

## August 11: Hero Within

We have conversations with ourself all the time. Some of the conversations are more useful than others. Conversations that tear down and criticize aren't helpful in bringing out our best golf.

A hero lives within us all. The hero that we find in our sanctuary is that part of us that deeply desires to do something of significance, be a person of character, and do marvelous things in golf.

Imagine that there are two chairs facing each other. Your current self is in one chair. In the other chair is your heroic self, who has grand aspirations and an abundance of courage. Take some time to be with your heroic self and ask her or him anything that's on your mind about golf or life in general.

***"I awaken the hero within me."***

## August 12: Home and Spirit

Our sanctuary is the natural home of our spirit, a place where we're most in touch with our own deep wisdom and the wisdom of the ages. When meditate in our sanctuary, we're practicing going "home." In time, we learn to recognize that, in our sanctuary, our spirit is free to be our best. We discover the part of us that's timeless and free—the part of us that feels the most like home to us.

As we continue to practice meditation and take time in our sanctuary, we increasingly bring our sanctuary and our spirit into our daily life. Our life and our golf game begin to be a different experience. We start playing and doing things in a way that's free, peaceful, and joyful.

***"I'm in touch with my sanctuary."***

## August 13: Finding Our Center

Our "center" is a metaphor for being in balance in life. Our center is a place where seeming opposites can live in harmony. For example, we can center ourself between caring about the outcome of a round versus not caring. We can center ourself about competing, competing with all of our focus and yet simply playing without becoming wrapped up in the competition.

Living from our center is a powerful way to be because we're able to live and play golf freely. We don't lock ourself into any one point of view about what we do. We're able to choose how we want to be in ways that are appropriate for what we want to accomplish.

***"I find my center."***

## August 14: Conversations With Spirit

We can have rich and powerful conversations with our spirit in our sanctuary. Our sanctuary is full of possibility and wisdom.

Imagine that you're in your sanctuary and that you're walking along a path. Everything is just the way you would want it to be. The scenery, the weather, and your state of mind are just as you want. You're walking along a path with your spirit. Spend some time with your spirit and talk about anything that comes to mind about life and golf.

***"I listen to my spirit."***

## August 15: Healthy Mind, Body, and Spirit

Health can affect our mind, body, and spirit. "Health" can mean different things to different people. There is objective data about what a healthy body means, but there's less consensus about what a healthy mind and spirit would be. Ultimately, we must decide for ourself what health means, and live and play in ways that are consistent with that.

Imagine how it would be for you to be healthy in mind, body, and spirit. In your sanctuary, imagine being healthy in every way and how that might look and feel. Imagine you're using golf as a way of being healthy. Imagine golf teaching you how to be healthier and freer.

***"I'm healthy in mind, body, and spirit."***

## August 16: Emotional Guidance

Emotions are an evaluation system. They help us navigate in life and golf. Emotions reflect our attitude about what's going on around us. They help us decide if things are good or bad, beautiful or ugly, and important or not important.

Emotions, just like thinking states, can have various depths to them. When we're deep in our sanctuary, our emotions take on a different quality as opposed to the emotions we feel when we're going about our daily lives. Both kinds of emotions have their purposes and are useful, but they are different. When we experience ourself feeling at a deep level in our sanctuary, the feelings have more of a long-term perspective and have timeless wisdom that accompanies them. We can trust that they can help us navigate our journey in golf over the years as we continue to play golf.

***"I pay attention to my deep emotions."***

## August 17: The Artist Spirit

For those of us who play golf more mechanically by focusing on swing thoughts, golf is something that we "do." We try to control our swings and our clubs. If things go well, then we feel successful. If things don't go well, then we can feel that we failed.

There's a different way to play golf from our spirit. Golf from our spirit is like an artist standing in front of a blank canvas. Rather than trying to force a piece of art to emerge, the artist just unleashes her creative energy, and the work of art creates itself.

There's a common saying we hear when golfers play well. They often say, "I just tried to get out of my own way." This saying reflects the artistic spirit in golf, where we just let go a bit and allow ourself the freedom to play golf.

***"I play golf artistically."***

## August 18: Passion

Golf won't turn out to be a way of making a living for most of us. However, if you love golf and still find yourself excited to play, then golf has taught you how it feels to be passionate about something, even if you're not making money doing it. Golf has given you a wonderful gift.

One characteristic of the spirit is a passion for something. Passion is personal and specific. What gives one person passion may do nothing for someone else. However, when people follow their passion, individuals, communities, and societies tend to benefit. Passion mobilizes people to be of service to many people in many different ways. What does your passion call you to do?

***"I follow my passion and accomplish great things."***

## August 19: Nature and Spirit

Nature has an incredible way of bringing us back to our spirit. Often we think of nature as something "out there," something that's separate and different from us as humans. That's because, in modern life, we spend most of our lives indoors. Most of us live and work indoors.

It's easy to feel separated from natural processes when so much of our lives are indoors, but we're still an integral part of nature. Just like all living creatures in nature, we experience the cycles of life and death. Nature has ways of reminding us that there are rhythms and cycles of life. She reminds us that we're here for a time to live fully and fruitfully. Hopefully, we leave things in better shape than when we found them so that the cycles of life can continue.

Golf takes us outside to feel the wind and the sun on our skin, breathe some fresh air, listen to the birds sing, and enjoy the magnificent movements of our bodies. Golf reminds us that we're a part of nature. We remember that it's good to be alive and be a force of nature.

***"Nature brings me back to my spirit."***

## August 20: Watching and Listening

To have access to the deep parts of us requires us to watch and listen. Deep wisdom doesn't have the same feel as solving a math problem or choosing between things. The deepest parts of us speak in a language of images, sensations, and emotions. The feeling is similar to being in a movie or dream.

Similar to a movie or dream, we must watch and listen. If we went to a movie theater and didn't watch and listen, we would have no experience of the movie. We watch and listen in order to experience our deeper wisdom.

Go to your sanctuary, to a place where you're in touch with your spirit. It's a place where only you and your spirit reside. Take some time to be there and be still. When you're ready, you can talk with your spirit about anything, just like you would talk to a dear old friend, who always understands you, but never judges.

***"I watch and listen."***

## August 21: Breathing Spirit

Breathing is a wonderful meditation technique. Being mindful of our breathing is a superb way of staying present, quieting our mind, and letting our mind rest.

Breathing into our spirit quiets our mind and awakens our spirit. Give your full attention to your inhalation and exhalation. As you continue to breathe, let your imagination go and imagine each breath awakening your spirit in your sanctuary. Imagine that you can see your spirit having bodily form and living in the world. What would it be doing? Imagine your spirit on the golf course. What would your spirit be doing there? What would it be feeling? What would your spirit be thinking?

***"I breathe into my spirit."***

## August 22: To Soar or Not

Soaring birds love a strong wind. All they need to do is stretch out their wings and let the wind lift them. The stronger the wind, the easier it is for the bird to soar, taking the bird higher and higher. Other non-soaring birds look for shelter or stand on the ground waiting for the wind to stop.

When strong winds come into our lives, we decide if we soar or look for shelter on the ground. Our spirit will call us to one or the other. Either choice can be a good one. Some spirits love to soar and live on the edge. Other' spirits want stability and predictability, waiting until conditions are more favorable for them to move.

The same principle applies in golf. Some people like to soar and live on the edge. Others prefer stability and predictability. The choice is ours.

***"I decide whether to soar or not."***

## August 23: Facing Dragons

Dragons are an ancient symbol of ferociousness, causing fear among even the most courageous. Knights went out, faced the dragons, and engaged them in battle. Only the most courageous and skillful could succeed.

What dragons await you in golf and life? Look inside of yourself and find the courage and skill that you need to face them. You have every resource and support that you need to succeed in your sanctuary. Imagine that you're so resourceful and strong that you can only succeed. Imagine that you're happy for the opportunity to show how strong and skillful you are.

***"I'm courageous every day."***

## August 24: Your Own Guru

There are wise people in the world, and we can learn much from them. However, it's equally true that we're also a potent source of wisdom. The problem is that many people don't take the time or have the meditative skills to listen deeply to themselves.

Imagine that you're in your sanctuary in a place where you're utterly relaxed and have a quiet mind. Imagine that there are two chairs facing each other. You're in one chair, and your guru-self—perhaps an older, wiser you—sits across from you. You can have a conversation with your guru-self.

Ask your guru-self how you can connect more with him or her. Ask your guru-self how you can move ahead in your golf game.

Ask him or her anything else that's on your mind. You may surprise yourself by the answers you receive.

***"I have the answers to the questions that I pose."***

## August 25: Playing With Spirit

Over the years, our bodies, our thinking, our emotions, and our values can change. Our spirit is constant. Our spirit is what makes us who we are, even as the circumstances in our lives change dramatically. There is a core of us which remains. Our spirit is the part of us that others who know us well recognize.

To play golf from our spirit is to play golf in total alignment with our true Self. Ego doesn't cloud the experience. We compete fully and purely for the joy and the experience of competition. We don't feel regret when things don't go as planned. We don't feel shame when our performance is below our capability. We don't gloat when we perform at a high level. We enjoy the moment and marvel at the wonders that our mind and body can perform.

***"I play golf with my spirit."***

## August 26: Peaceful Spirit

Some people have to give up golf because it frustrates them too much, or they don't want to deal with the ups and downs of golf. That's reasonable. Why do things that make us miserable?

Another approach is to treat golf as a means for learning to be peaceful. We can find peace in knowing that golfing excellence is a journey and not a destination. In our sanctuary, we find a part of us that's peaceful about life and golf. Our Egos have a lot invested in achieving results right now and feeling successful. Our spirit is open to being in a process of development, being on a journey, and letting events unfold in their proper times.

***"I'm a peaceful golfer."***

## August 27: Being Joyful

We can play and understand golf as a spiritual activity that speaks to a deep part of us. Golf can help liberate us from self-induced suffering to full lives that are characterized by joyfulness. One of the sure signs of spiritual growth is joyfulness.

Those who are spiritually growing may not be changing the circumstances of their lives or their golf games. Those who are spiritually growing are changing their perspectives about their lives and their golf games. They come to understand themselves more fully, and live their lives and play golf in ways that are more consistent with who they are in their sanctuary. As a result, their lives are more consistent, meaningful, and joyful.

***"I'm joyful as I practice and play."***

## August 28: Magical

Most kids believe that life is magical. They deeply believe that wonderful things should happen all the time. When we grow up, most of us lose the sense that life is magical and that marvelous and unexpected things can and do occur. Magic is a metaphor for extraordinary things being possible in life. Magic is also a metaphor for personal power. We're all capable of magical things if we believe and apply ourselves to something with our whole heart.

If you've lost your magic in golf, you can find it again. Start believing in your magic again. Start believing that you're powerful again. Start believing that strange and wonderful things can happen if you believe in yourself and give yourself fully to your dreams.

***"I'm magical."***

## August 29: Spiritual Symbols

Symbols and metaphors are the language of the subconscious. Our dreams are the most potent example of the language of the subconscious. We usually shouldn't take our dreams literally, but as symbols of some messages that the deeper parts of us are trying to communicate to us. Similarly, we don't take symbols literally. We have to interpret what they mean. Symbols can also mean different things to different people.

Symbols that catch our attention or resonate with us are trying to communicate with us at a deep level, to help us along in golf and life by helping us focus on the right things. What symbols of golf interest you? Some golfers wear colors of clothing or styles of clothing. Some golfers have rituals that they perform. Other golfers or people who we admire can be symbols for us. They might be a symbol of excellence or perseverance or creativity. Trophies, championships, awards, and honors can be symbols of excellence. The number and range of symbols that we might find appealing are endless. What are your symbols of golfing excellence?

***"I pay attention to meaningful symbols."***

## August 30: Feeling the Sanctuary

As we progress in the ability to meditate and go deeper into our sanctuary, we become more familiar with how we feel at a deep level. Our sanctuary teaches us how it feels when we are in touch with our spirit. Many people feel peacefulness, joy, and well-being.

As you go deeper into your sanctuary, notice how you feel. Over time, you'll be able to experience the same feelings more often in your daily life and as you play golf. Imagine how your golf game would be if you played with the same feelings that you experience in your sanctuary. That's the power and beauty of the sanctuary.

***"I pay attention to my spiritual feelings."***

## August 31: Thinking With Spirit

Learning meditation is about becoming more powerful, centered, and peaceful. When we practice meditation, we're developing the power to choose what and how we think.

Spend some time in your sanctuary noticing your thinking. Many people find their thinking in their sanctuary to be abundantly clear, focused, and imaginative. The sanctuary is a particularly rich environment for using our imagination. The more time we give to imaginative thinking in our sanctuary, the greater is our ability to do that same thinking in our daily lives and as we play golf.

***"I think with my spirit."***

# *September: Being Healthy*

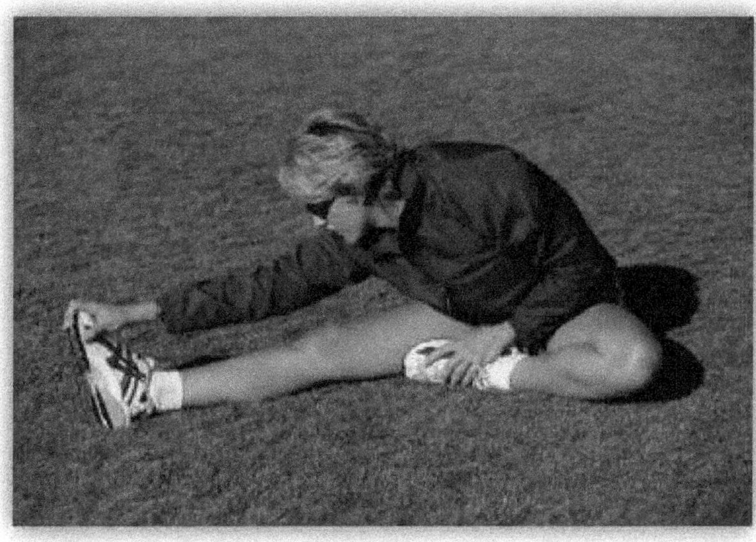

Sports remind us that we're both mind and body and that we have to take care of both to perform our best. A healthy mind focuses on the present because it has freed itself from unnecessary burdens. A healthy body is rested, strong, flexible, and responsive to what we ask of it.

## September 1: Free and Healthy

Being healthy is largely a matter of always moving toward freedom. Complete the following sentences as spontaneously as possible with as many endings as possible. Record your answers for further reflection.

- I could be freer if...
- The things that keep me from being freer are...
- The things that help me be freer are...
- I will be freer when...
- What I need to be freer are...
- To be freer, I need to start...
- To be freer, I need to stop...
- The things I don't understand about being freer are...
- Sources of freedom for me might be...
- If I were totally free, I would...

Imagine living in ways that are freer in mind and body. Imagine making the decision to be freer. Imagine helping others to be freer.

***"I'm free and healthy."***

## September 2: Eating Healthily

For athletes to be at our best physically and mentally, we need to take care of our bodies. Our diet significantly affects both mental and physical activities. Most of us understand the physical impacts of poor food choices. Some of us underestimate the impact of food on the quality of our thinking. However, we need only reflect on our experience to know that our food affects our thinking.

Reflect on times when you've eaten poorly or gone without food while playing golf or doing some other physical activity. How was your thinking? Likely, your thinking became clouded, and your decision-making skills suffered because when we go without food for too long, our mind goes into fight or flight mode. When we're in a fight or flight mode, the problem-solving part of our brain activates rather than staying in an imaginative state of mind that we require to play our best.

On the other hand, when we eat food that is too rich and heavy, our natural tendency is to slow down and even go to sleep. This is obviously not an optimal state of mind and body for athletic performance.

Learning to appreciate healthy food is a choice that we make. Imagine eating many different healthy foods and truly enjoying them. Imagine how you'll look and feel. Imagine taking healthy snacks with you to the golf course and when you work out, keeping your mind and body sharp and ready to perform.

***"I eat healthy food in the right proportions."***

## September 3: Exercising

The right exercise is essential for keeping our mind and body working well together. Many people think of exercise as only a physical activity. However, exercise is also a mental discipline. When we exercise in the right ways, we quiet our mind and center ourself. The feeling we have is often one of well-being as we enjoy what our body can do and appreciate our body's skillful movements.

If we exercise with our analytical mind racing, the feeling is usually one of "working hard" at exercise. Exercise is best when we let go of the need to analyze and problem-solve and just enjoy the quiet of our mind.

If you struggle with motivation for exercising, begin with some imaginative work on how good it will feel when you're fit, healthy, and moving the way you want.

Consult with training professionals about an exercise program that is right for you.

***"I exercise in ways that fit me."***

## September 4: Stretching

Flexibility is central to performance in golf. Especially as we age, time has a way of decreasing our flexibility if we don't actively work at maintaining it. The process of losing flexibility is often almost imperceptible.

Many great resources are available to suggest stretches that are appropriate for golf. Many people find yoga a helpful discipline. In addition, certified trainers can suggest programs for individual needs.

There's a mental component to stretching, as there is a mental component for all aspects of sports and fitness. Imagine you're faithful to a stretching regimen. Imagine you maintain flexibility throughout your life. Imagine being highly motivated to stretch.

***"I stretch appropriately every day."***

## September 5: Healthy Warm Up

Warm-up includes a mental and physical component. It's a time to get our mind and body in sync. A mental warm-up can begin before you even leave home. Begin by imagining how you want your mind and body to function together. Imagine you're feeling loose and relaxed, playing just the way you want. Imagine you're feeling healthy and strong because you've taken care of your mind and body with adequate stretching, a good diet, and deep sleep. Imagine you're making great swings, chips, and putts.

Imagine you're playing with a quiet, confident mind. You focus well and have a terrific time playing.

Later, while you warm up on the range, use affirmations to continue warming up mentally as you also warm up physically. Say positive things to yourself. Affirm how healthy you are and what a talented player you are, mentally and physically.

***"I warm up my mind and body before I play."***

## September 6: Feeling Good

Being healthy doesn't require perfection. No one's body or mind is perfect. What's important is that we accept our imperfections. Feeling good about ourself can be as straightforward as acknowledging that we're a work in progress, which is true of any of us. None of us is perfect and yet we're learning, growing, and doing the best we can.

We decide how we feel about ourself by deciding what we focus on about ourself and how we choose to interpret that data about ourself. Why not choose to accept that we're a work in progress and feel good about that? There's no downside to feeling good about ourself.

***"I'm a work in progress."***

## September 7: Letting Go of Stress

Part of being healthy in mind and body is avoiding undue stress. Stress is a learned reaction. We can also unlearn stress. Once we're an adult, we're responsible for choosing what stresses us out or doesn't stress us out.

Some golfers feel stress on the golf course. Stress goes beyond feeling pressure and tension. We can learn to perform while feeling pressure or tension, but stress makes it difficult to perform on the golf course.

To learn to manage stress, we need to become sensitive to where stress shows up in our body. When you feel stress, notice where you feel it in your body. Some people feel stress as tightness in their shoulders or neck. The feelings of stress can show up anywhere in your body. Take note of where stress shows up in your body. Notice what the feeling is. Most people feel it as tightness, but the feeling can vary with individuals.

From your sanctuary, remember times when you felt wonderful and how that felt. When you feel wonderful, where do you feel that in your body? Some people feel lightness in their chest as they breathe. Others feel their facial muscles relaxing. It varies with individuals. Take note of where you feel the sensations in your body. Now imagine bringing that wonderful feeling to the place where you normally feel stress. Imagine the wonderful feeling replacing the feeling of stress. Imagine the wonderful feeling intensifying and spreading throughout your body until your whole body feels healthy and strong.

Imagine living your life in the future with less stress or no stress. Imagine being peaceful as you accept challenges in life, knowing that you're capable and will figure out what to do about any challenge. Imagine letting go of the things you can't control.

***"I eliminate stress from my life."***

## September 8: Deep Sleep

Sleep is crucial for athletes. We can't be at our best if our mind and body are weary. The importance of resting our body is common knowledge. However, fewer of us understand the need to rest our mind. Our mind becomes weary if we're in constant problem-solving mode. It can feel as if our mind is working 24x7.

Good, deep sleep comes from being able to quiet our mind. People who have active analytical minds that can't let go have a difficult time sleeping. Their mind keeps racing, which also keeps their body from fully relaxing. The mind and the body are a system. If our mind is vigilant, our body will be vigilant and vice versa. If our mind relaxes, our body relaxes.

The first step towards deep sleep is to meditate on an affirmation such as the following every night. We need to begin to program our mind regarding the intention of letting go and having deep sleep. As you meditate on the affirmation in your sanctuary bedroom, imagine you're letting go of any concerns so that your mind and body can rest.

***"I sleep deeply every night."***

## September 9: Future Being

Adults can choose who we want to be. There's no script or fate to follow. We can write the story any way we choose. That includes deciding who we are as golfers, athletes, and people. When we decide who we are in our sanctuary, what we do in golf and life starts to change. What we do flows from who we are.

It may take some time and work to transform ourself into who we want to be, but it begins with a vision. Complete the following sentences as spontaneously as possible with as many endings as possible. Record your answers for further reflection.

- When I think about my dreams as a golfer, I hope...
- My life would be extremely interesting if...

- In the back of my mind, I have always wondered about being...
- What I care about deeply are...
- If I had no reservations, I would...
- I think my life would be entirely fulfilling by...
- If I could start over right now, I would...
- I had always hoped that my life would be...
- If I had no fear, I would...

Pay close attention to the responses that you feel are the most surprising or emotional as you read them. Imagine in the future being who you truly desire to be and how that would be. Imagine how that could lead to a healthy lifestyle.

***"I begin today to be the person I choose to be."***

## September 10: Social and Private

Being healthy in mind and body is largely about achieving balance. Being a healthy human being, in part, means that we find balance between the social and private aspects of life. Golf, just like the rest of life, has both social and private aspects to it.

Some people energize themselves with social gatherings. Others energize themselves by being alone. Both are fine. Whatever our preference is, it's good to stretch ourself and experience the breadth of human experience. Maturing is learning to appreciate different facets of life. Maturity is a movement to balance.

Golf is an excellent time to be both social and alone. See if you can find yourself enjoying both aspects more.

***"I enjoy the social and private aspects of golf."***

## September 11: Recovering

Research in medicine continues to support what many of us know from our own experience that there's a relationship between our thinking and our health. Healthy thinking promotes physical health.

The first step towards recovery from injury or illness is to get proper treatment from health care professionals. After that, our job is to engage our mind in the recovery process. We want to create a mind-set that we're becoming healthier and stronger every day. That begins by imagining ourself becoming healthier and stronger every day.

Imagine all the cells of your body working together to keep you strong and healthy. Imagine feeling highly motivated and doing the kinds of rehabilitation that your health care professionals prescribe for you. Imagine going through your days with only positive, helpful, life-giving thoughts. You think and feel healthier every day. You've given up the bad habits of negative thinking—only positive thoughts from here forward. You let go of stress and live in the present in peace.

Injury or illness can be a good opportunity to take a step back and reevaluate what we believe and what we're doing. Resolve to come away from injury or illness even stronger, surer, and more confident about the direction you're heading. During your recovery, you can meditate even more.

***"I'm healthier in mind and body each day."***

## September 12: Acceptance

Much of golf involves learning to accept "what is." A round of golf is never perfect. Some of us spend a lot of energy wishing things were different from what they are. To live in a place where we constantly wish things were other than they are is to live in conflict and disappointment. Self-acceptance opens us up to the possibility of much greater peace and joy in our life and golf game.

Golf can teach us a good deal about acceptance and self-acceptance. We're the ones who decide to accept things, both good and bad, as they are today. That doesn't mean that we shouldn't work to change things that we can change for the better, but that activity has its own proper time and place. At the moment, things are what they are—a bad shot is a bad shot. Accept that it happened, let it go and move forward. It's up to us to make the choice. Living with acceptance can be a healthy, peaceful way to live and play golf.

***"I live with acceptance."***

## September 13: Mind Vacations

Our mind gets tired, just like our body. Those with active minds sometimes feel as if there are constant internal conversations going on in their minds. It can be exhausting to have continuous internal conversations.

Learning to quiet our mind by meditation helps us to be able to quiet our mind when we need to rest. Golf helps us learn how to do that. We recognize the need for a quiet mind in golf. Then we practice being quiet on the golf course. Then we apply the practice to other aspects of our life when appropriate.

Go to your sanctuary and imagine being in a vacation place where you can deeply relax, where you haven't a care in the world. Imagine how your mind quiets as you relax in that place, perhaps taking a walk or sitting on a beach or watching a sunset. Let go of the need for internal conversation and just be present to how it feels to relax completely. It's good to quiet your mind when you want.

***"I take mind vacations."***

## September 14: Healthy Self

Some people have images of themselves as susceptible to injury or illness. The image we have of ourself may or may not have anything to do with reality. It's simply our understanding of who we are and the stories that we retell others and ourself. We can change the image we have of ourself. Sometimes simply changing the image we have of ourself is enough to change who we are and what we do.

If your self-image is one susceptible to injury or illness, it's time to let go of that image and create an image of yourself as healthy and strong from this day forward. From your sanctuary, imagine being a healthy and strong person. Imagine what you would be doing, how it would feel, and how your thinking would be different. Imagine you're growing even stronger in your identity as a healthy person. Imagine you're completely healthy for the rest of your long and joyful life. Imagine how good it is to live and play golf that way.

***"I'm a healthy person."***

## September 15: Living With Appreciation

Healthy minds begin with healthy thoughts. An exceptionally healthy thought is to live with appreciation. To appreciate something is the ability to find something good in it. If we appreciate our lives and our golf games for what they are now and take stock of what's good about them, then we have the ability to live and play golf with appreciation. Living with appreciation makes it possible to believe that we're good golfers, that we're good people and that we can live in peace with others and ourself.

Think about the most appreciative people you've ever known, the ones who just seemed to enjoy almost everything and everyone. How was it to be around them? Imagine that you can see through their eyes and know their thoughts. How might you change if you develop the ability to live with deep appreciation? How might that change your golf game?

***"I appreciate everything more each day."***

## September 16: Passive Observer

Our mind wants something to do on the golf course between shots. We want to give our mind something to do to relax because being on the golf course for four hours or more with total concentration is exhausting. Being healthy is making choices that are consistent with what keeps us fresh and ready to perform without draining our tank physically, mentally, or emotionally.

Some people relax by talking to others, which is good if both people enjoy that way of relaxing. Others prefer to be quiet in their own private space. You can be quiet in your own private space by simply becoming a passive observer of what's going on around you.

Between shots, try passively noticing what's going on around you without analyzing or critiquing. The hard part of being an observer is to be passive and not engage our analytical ability. See how long you can observe without analyzing or critiquing.

***"I'm a passive observer when I want to be."***

## September 17: Joyful Exercise

Our attitude and our focus during exercise affect the quality of the experience. If we convince ourself that exercising is going to be hard, and we focus on the parts of exercise that are hard, it will be hard. Our attitude largely determines whether the experience will be enjoyable or not.

There are ways of enjoying exercise—to the point where exercising can be joyful. One approach is to focus on the parts of exercise that are pleasant. If you're outside, you can notice nature, the feeling of air on your skin, or the feeling of air filling and leaving your lungs.

Another approach is that you can let your mind drift to a place that's far away and unrelated to exercise. You can have a place in your sanctuary where you relax, things are easy, and your body moves with ease. Have your mind stay there while you exercise.

You can also create an expectation of well-being prior to exercising. Imagine exercising and fully enjoying the experience. Imagine appreciating how enjoyable it feels to be able to use your body in a healthy, skillful manner.

***"I enjoy exercise more each day."***

## September 18: Deciding to Sleep Well

Some people don't sleep well simply because they have not made a quality decision to sleep well. Some people have subconsciously decided to problem-solve while they are in bed, thinking about what has happened during the day and what will happen in the future. It's fine if we problem-solve at night in bed on rare occasions, but as a lifestyle, it's a formula for exhaustion.

In your sanctuary, in a place where you're in touch with your past, remember a decision that you made in your life that was a good decision. You knew it at the time that it was a good decision. Notice at that time how it felt to make the decision. Try to remember how it felt in your body to make a good decision. Some people feel warmth in their chest or gut. The feeling varies with individuals.

Now bring that same feeling and quality of decision-making to your decision to sleep well. Feel the same feelings. Imagine feeling just as sure about your decision to sleep well from now on.

***"I have decided to sleep well from now on."***

## September 19: Joy of Confidence

Joy is the soul mate of confidence. When we feel truly confident, we usually feel joyful. Feeling confidence and joy as we play golf is a wonderful way of keeping our performance free and flowing, without the tension that creeps in when we invest too much of the wrong kinds of energy in our game. When we invest our Ego in our performance, it feels that we're performing from a place of fear or need.

One way of judging whether you're a confident golfer or not is by the amount of joy you feel when you play. How joyful are you when you play? Imagine how it would be if you were confident and joyful as you play, even in intense matches or tournaments. See and feel yourself in the near future being confident and joyful as you play. Imagine playing in all sorts of circumstances and feeling joy every minute of it.

***"I experience great joy in golf."***

## September 20: Holding On and Letting Go

Health is about letting go of some things and holding on to other things. With golf, we want to have a selective memory, remembering the best and letting go of the rest. Learning lessons from mistakes or disappointments is vital, but once we learn them, we let them go.

We decide how much "space" we give to the past in our mind. Some people have given the past so much space that there's little or no room for the present or future. They define and limit themselves by their past. We simply have to decide how much space we allow anything in our mind.

We learn to manage the space in our mind by going to our sanctuary and consciously choosing what draws our attention in meditation.

***"I manage the space in my mind."***

## September 21: Healthy Now

When does health begin for us? Does health begin soon, tomorrow, next week, or after the New Year? If we're honest with ourself, being healthy always begins right now. We want to have a sense of our future direction and goals because they provide direction to the present. However, health begins right now. Health begins with our next choice. What can you do today that will promote your health now and in the future?

Imagine you focus more on your health as a lifestyle. Imagine you're more conscious of your desire to eat well, exercise, rest, meditate, spend time in quality social situations and take care of your spirit. Imagine you feel passion for being healthy, while looking and feeling better each day.

***"I have a great passion for being healthy."***

## September 22: Breathing

Golf teaches us the importance of breathing. When we're nervous or feeling under pressure, the tendency is to hold our breath or breathe shallowly. Holding our breath starves our muscles and our mind of needed oxygen. That creates even more tension and poor decision-making.

As straightforward as it sounds, breathing is a key for maintaining health by feeding our mind and body needed oxygen. We have to train ourself to breathe deeply, even when it goes against natural tendencies.

Imagine being on the golf course in what would be a pressure situation for you. Imagine breathing deeply and feeling tension flow out of your mind and body. Imagine developing the habit of breathing deeply on the golf course. Imagine having deep breathing as part of your pre-shot and putting routines.

***"I focus on deep breathing every day."***

## September 23: Re-creating Yourself

We can think of the word recreation as meaning "re-creation." When we re-create, it's as if we are starting fresh, beginning anew. Golf is a terrific teacher of how to re-create. Mostly, re-creation is a letting go of the highly analytical lives that most of us live in the twenty-first century. We have many ways of keeping ourselves busy and distracted. Maintaining that lifestyle takes large amounts of energy.

Re-creation is about letting go of the analytical and getting back in touch with our body and spirit. Golf is about enjoying competition and nature, and at its core, it's about play. Play gets us back in touch with our body and spirit.

***"I take time to re-create myself."***

## September 24: Your Physical Ability

We choose our attitude toward our body and physical ability. Our attitude towards our body and physical ability either enables or impedes our ability to perform as an athlete. Golf teaches us that if we believe that we're not able to hit a shot or make a putt, we most likely won't be able to do it.

From your sanctuary, remember a time when you felt highly confident in your physical ability. It doesn't have to be associated with golf or even a sport. Remember how you looked and especially how you felt. Remember the physical sensations of movement and coordination. Try to remember what your thinking might have been at that point.

If you can't remember a time when you believed in your physical ability, imagine how it might have been to believe completely in your physical ability. Imagine what your thinking might have been if you felt that way. Now imagine playing golf with those same beliefs and even more so.

***"I believe in my physical ability."***

## September 25: Spiritually Rich

Being healthy includes being healthy in our spirit, which means that deep down we're at peace and we connect with what we believe to be important and having lasting value. We're deeply in touch with our wisdom and connect with others in rich and meaningful ways. To be "spiritually rich" is to live in a way that goes beyond surface meanings and appearances. Our subconscious mind gives us glimpses into the things that go beyond surface meanings and appearances. Our imagination helps us connect with the deeper parts of our mind and spirit in our sanctuary. Some of us connect with our Higher Power in our sanctuary.

Imagine how it would be for you to connect increasingly well with the deeper parts of your mind and spirit in your sanctuary. You're in touch with your deep wisdom. You understand yourself and others in a way that's deep and meaningful. When you connect with your spiritual self, life becomes rich, interesting, and meaningful.

***"I'm spiritually rich."***

## September 26: Being Better

To be healthy is to be on a path towards improvement. Aging doesn't have to be a process of decline. If we take care of ourself physically, mentally, and spiritually, we can experience longer and higher quality lives that were unimaginable for past generations. Although we will experience physical changes as we age, many parts of our lives can improve with age. We can live more healthily. We can experience the great joys of maturity, self-discovery, and gain knowledge about how life works. That brings us more choice, more influence in the world, more peace with others and within ourself, and a greater sense of fulfillment.

Imagine you're improving throughout your life in all dimensions. Imagine being just the way you want to be.

***"I choose to become better throughout my life."***

## September 27: Living Out Metaphors

Health is, in large part, a series of good choices. Some things are out of our control, but many things are within our control. There are the larger choices that we make about who we are and how we live that take years to play out. There are also smaller but no less serious choices that we make that determine the course of our day, week, and month.

We can think about our choices in terms of metaphors because we can understand them easily, and they speak to our imagination and subconscious mind. These metaphors can help guide our choices to be more consistent and predictable. Some common metaphors that people live out are the following: the saint, the warrior, the athlete, the father, the mother, the king, the queen, the jester, the leader, the follower, the champion, the top gun, the monk, the wizard, and the prophet. Do any of these metaphors appeal to you as a model for how to live life and play golf? Perhaps you have your own metaphor.

Some people have nicknames that they have adopted or created which are another type of metaphor. Some people have alter egos that are also a type of metaphor. Some people relate to superheroes or characters in movies. At your depths, what metaphors are you living? Imagine how it would be to live and play golf in a way that more fully expresses your deep desires.

***"I understand myself by the metaphors that I'm living."***

## September 28: Mind and Body

Some people understand themselves primarily in terms of how they think. Others understand themselves primarily in terms of how they feel. However, we're both mind and body. We want our mind and body working together in harmony. We want to care for our body just as much as we care for our mind.

Golf reminds us of the need to have our mind and body working well together. Golf teaches us how it is when our mind and body work well together and when they don't work well together. There are times when our mind has a clear vision of the swing that we want to make, but our body isn't able to do what we want. There are times when our body is ready to perform, but our mind isn't thinking in the right ways to allow us to perform. Then there are times when our mind and body connect well and are ready to perform.

Notice how it is when your mind and body are performing well together. Notice what you did to help that connection. Was there any pre-round warm-up or routine that helped? How did you sleep the night before you performed well? What did you eat? Did you do some mental warm-up before you came to the golf course? What meditation did you do? Keep noticing and figuring out what helps your mind and body work well together.

***"I take care of my mind and body."***

## September 29: Mental Ability

Go to a place in your sanctuary where you're in touch with your past. Remember a time when you felt highly confident in your mental ability. It doesn't have to be a golf or sports memory. Remember how it was to trust your thinking. Try to remember what your thinking was at that point. If you can't remember a time when you felt highly confident in your mental ability, imagine how it might have been to feel that way. Imagine what your thinking might have been.

Now imagine playing golf with that same ability and even more. You have all the mental ability you need to play extraordinary golf and to live an extraordinary life. You use your analytical and imaginative abilities perfectly. You're in the flow of the game, performing at your highest ability.

***"I fully believe in my mental ability."***

## September 30: Being Complete

Those who live peacefully and confidently have a sense that they are complete in the present. There's nothing they need right now to make them complete. They have no obsession with things needing to be something other than they are right now. It doesn't mean that they are perfect and have everything imaginable in the world at their disposal, but it means that they have fundamentally accepted that they lack nothing in the present. Things will change in the future, but they are complete in the present.

Being healthy is in large part about deciding to be complete right now. That's not to say that there aren't times when we want to change things about our situation or ourself. Some things take time and effort to change. If that's the case, then we can accept that some changes take time to unfold, and we accept that we're complete right now.

Imagine being complete right now. Imagine letting go of anything that causes you to feel you're not complete right now. Imagine living in a way that's complete, more often. Imagine playing each round of golf feeling that you're complete and have everything you need to play well right now.

***"I choose to be complete right now."***

# *October: Being a Great Short Gamer*

About two-thirds of the shots in a round are short shots and putts. We don't shoot low scores without having a reasonable short game. Having a great short game begins with the recognition of the importance of the short game. Then we have to commit to practicing, both mentally and physically.

## October 1: Where to Focus

Complete the following sentences as spontaneously as possible with as many endings as possible. Record your answers for further reflection.

- The parts of my short game that are excellent are...
- The things that frustrate me the most in my short game are...
- In my short game, I feel the most nervous when...
- In my short game, I feel the most relaxed when...
- In the past, my biggest struggles with putting have been...
- In the past, my biggest struggles with chipping have been...
- The parts of my short game that used to be good are...
- The most important things about the short game are...
- If I knew I could become highly skilled in my short game, I would...
- I feel like my emotions help me in my short game when...
- I feel like my emotions cause me trouble in my short game when...
- With my short game, I truly don't like feeling...
- In my short game, I trust...
- In my short game, I don't trust...

Pay attention to the responses that are the strongest or the most surprising. Your answers will be a mix of things you do well and things that need improvement. See if you can categorize your answers and identify the highest priority items to improve.

***"I understand what I need to improve."***

## October 2: Right Mental Approach

To be skilled in the short game, we need more than solid short-game mechanics. We also need a solid mental approach. The right mental approach is working on feel, concentrating on targets, and playing freely when it matters the most. The right mental approach is to imagine ourself being a champion even before we step onto the golf course to play. We have already mentally put ourself in a position to win because of the way we have prepared.

The right mental approach for practice is to engage your imagination by mentally imagining yourself in game situations. If you're chipping, imagine yourself in various game situations, trying to simulate in your mind what you might think and feel. Imagine needing to get up and down to win a hole or to win a tournament. Imagine that there's a crowd watching you, so you have to focus even more intently on what you're doing. Imagine you're thoroughly enjoying having a chance to win a tournament, feeling no pressure at all while having fun in that situation. Imagine needing to make putts to continue a match or stay in a tournament.

***"I use my imagination as I practice."***

## October 3: Components of Putting

We have to manage our physical state and mental state while putting. Managing our physical state is how we want our body to feel when putting. This can entail feelings in our fingers, hands, forearms, shoulders, neck, back, legs, feet, and even facial muscles. What's the feeling that you want in your body before, during, and after you putt? Most people prefer to feel their muscles relaxed, but the exact physical feelings depend on personal preference. For example, if grip pressure is a key physical feeling for you, then you must determine through practice just how much grip pressure feels good. You must also decide where you feel grip pressure specifically. Is one hand more important than the other is? Is it in one finger, some fingers, or all fingers? Do you feel the right pressure in a part of a finger?

Managing our mental state while putting includes what we think and feel, emotionally, about a putt. What works best for you? Do you perform best when you're calm, attentive, peaceful, vigilant, or alert? Do you perform best when you say positive things to yourself, or just imagine the target, or feel the tempo of the stroke? Individuals will vary with what works best for them. You'll have to experiment and find what works best for you.

***"I manage my physical and mental states while putting."***

## October 4: Putting Imaginatively

Playing golf with a quiet mind is a critical skill to acquire. Learning to putt with a quiet mind is even more so. Studies have shown that players who putt poorly overuse the analytical part of their brain. Players who putt well use the imaginative part of their brain.

Our mind wants something to do while putting, so we either focus on a target or pay attention to the feeling in our body as we putt. Both putting to a target and putting with feel are imaginative activities. Neither activity shifts our mind into analytical mode. Contrast this with the analytical mode of putting. Analytical putters consider the consequences of missing putts. They pose the following kinds of questions to themselves. How embarrassed will I be if I miss this short putt? What if I don't make this birdie putt? How bad will I feel if I roll this putt four feet past the hole and miss the next putt? How devastating would it be if I four-putted a green? If miss this putt, am I going to lose the tournament? This style of thinking shifts the analytical part of the brain into high gear. With this kind of analytical thinking, we are inviting failure and entertaining it in our imagination.

***"I putt with a quiet mind."***

## October 5: Great Short Game

Some people mistakenly believe that they will become confident golfers once they develop their ability sufficiently. That's placing the cart before the horse. Sustainable confidence precedes performance, especially in the short game. Confidence fuels the fire of improvement.

Begin by believing in your ability to master your short game. Imagine sitting in your sanctuary movie theater watching yourself on the screen in the future. You have an excellent short game—pitching, chipping, and putting. You're hitting shots and putts just the way you want.

Now intensify the images and colors in the movie so that everything is bright, large, and attractive. Now, intensify the sounds, emotions, and sensations in the movie in a pleasing way.

After a few minutes of watching, imagine becoming part of the movie. Now feel how it is to have such wonderful short game skills. Imagine what your thinking will be when you have such a wonderful short game.

***"I'm mastering my short game."***

## October 6: Putting to Targets

Ideally, we want to putt as automatically as possible as if putting were as routine as tying our shoes. That's the goal—putt automatically. When we putt automatically, we let the wisdom of our mind and body skillfully do what we have trained so hard for them to do.

When we start putting automatically, we fill our imagination with the target only and allow the wisdom of our subconscious to coordinate our mind and body.

Putting is a good place to begin playing automatically to targets because the putting stroke is simple compared to the full golf swing or chipping stroke. Begin with putting and learn to play automatically to targets.

***"I putt automatically to my targets."***

## October 7: Putting to Tempo

Another good way to be present and putt with a quiet mind is to putt to tempo. Putting to tempo is uncomplicated and highly effective. All we need to do is to say silently "tick" and "tock" during the putting stroke. We say, "tick" when we begin the backstroke and "tock" when we make impact with the ball. When you say the words, imagine that you can hear yourself saying the words aloud. We don't use numbers such as "1" and "2" to work on tempo because numbers tend to activate the analytical part of our mind.

Experiment with the tempo of your stroke to find what works best for you. Some players feel comfortable with slower tempos. Other players feel comfortable with faster tempos. What matters is that you find a tempo that feels good, is repeatable, and produces your desired results most of the time.

***"I putt with great tempo."***

## October 8: Adverse Conditions

It's pleasurable to practice our short game in perfect conditions. It feels terrific, and we usually perform better than we would in poor conditions. If we played golf only in perfect conditions, that would make golf easier to master. Learn to appreciate practicing and playing in adverse conditions. Practice when it's windy, rainy, hot, or cold. Practice when the course conditions are difficult, and the lies aren't perfect. Practicing in adverse conditions is especially pertinent with the short game because the short-game shots tend to be so precise and feel-oriented.

Learn to believe in your ability to play in adverse conditions. Your mental and physical practice builds a competitive advantage. Rather than dreading playing in adverse conditions, you can learn to appreciate them.

***"I practice in adverse conditions."***

## October 9: Short Game Imagination

A strong imagination is the key to an effective short game. A strong imagination is the doorway to creativity around the greens. There's a great deal of room for creativity in the short game. There are many lies that we might have around the green. We can use many different clubs around the green. A strong imagination can suspend disbelief of what's reasonable or possible. If we're simply doing what others are doing, then we're not using our imagination. We're imitating. Someone had to be the first one to hit a flop shot. Someone had to be the first one to chip with a fairway metal. Now they have become a regular part of many players' games.

Bring that same attitude to your short-game practice. Use your imagination and trust your creativity.

***"I have a wonderful imagination."***

## October 10: Feeling the Short Game

People with a strong preference for analytical thinking will try to make the short game mechanical and "scientific." This is how the yips get into putting—overusing the analytical part of our mind. While mechanics matter in the short game, mechanics are secondary to feel. For some people, developing a good short game will be learning to discover feel. It may sound strange to say that golfers will "discover" their feel, but being aware of our physical sensations is a skill that most of us have to develop to some degree. Some people have more sensitivity to feel, but everyone can learn to develop their sense of feel.

***"I feel my short game."***

## October 11: Perfecting Shots

Putting and some of the short shots around the green are technically some of the simpler parts of golf. The putting stroke is mechanically the simplest of all strokes in golf. However, mastery in the short game doesn't come from being technically perfect. Mastery comes from learning to hit different shots around the green. Once we have developed a reasonable level of mechanics in the short game, it's time to work on hitting different kinds of shots with different clubs.

See how many shots you can create around the green. Seve Ballesteros used to practice with a 3-iron around the green and in bunkers because he wanted to force himself to be creative. What new shots can you learn?

***"I love to learn and perfect different short-game shots."***

## October 12: Short-Game Guru

Go to your sanctuary, to a place where you can have a conversation with a short-game guru. Imagine there are two chairs facing each other. Your present self sits in one chair. A short-game guru sits in the other chair. The guru is you in the future. Your future guru-self discovered some great secrets about the short game, about practice, and about the mental side of the short game. Discuss how you can improve your short game with your guru-self. Perhaps you'll surprise yourself by what you learn.

***"I learn from my short-game guru."***

## October 13: Up and Down

The "up and down" in golf is where the player gets his or her ball into the hole from off the green in two shots, most often by chipping, and then putting. The "up and down" is the highlight of a round because it means that we're chipping well and putting well. Since two-thirds of the shots in a golf game are the short-game variety, it means that if we're getting up and down regularly, we're likely shooting decent scores. Getting up and down also takes some pressure off our ball striking. We believe that we can get the ball up and down without hitting the ball perfectly all day.

Confidence is central in the short game. Confidence begins by imagining ourself getting the ball up and down. On your sanctuary golf course, imagine you're getting up and down from as many positions on the course as you can. Imagine you're making great chips, pitches, and putts, one after another. Imagine you're creative with your short game, feeling highly confident. Imagine you have a strong short game that's always there for you. Imagine your short game has become the strength of your game. Imagine you're playing with a high-confidence level, previously unknown to you.

***"I get the ball up and down from anywhere."***

## October 14: Wedges and Putter

Golfers have relationships with their clubs. They are an extension of us. We may like some of our clubs more than others because we have hit many good shots or putts with them. Similarly, we may dislike some clubs because we have hit enough foul shots to lose confidence in the clubs.

In the coming days and weeks, resolve to start liking your wedges and putter more because you're going to hit many superb shots and putts. Imagine that once you start believing in your wedges and putter, they will start to perform excellently for you. Confidence precedes performance. Believe that your wedges and putter will become your favorite clubs because you save so many strokes with them. Make the decision to improve your short game. Make the decision that your short game will be the strength of your game. Make the decision to appreciate your short-game clubs.

***"I truly appreciate my short-game clubs."***

## October 15: A Rollback Plan

We're always learning in golf. We can learn something from every round if we're paying attention. Some insights prove to be worthwhile over the long run, others don't. Some insights seem to be useful for a while and then stop being useful as if they have an expiration date. The short game can involve a lot of learning and experimentation because there's potentially so much room for creativity.

For those who have a large appetite for learning and experimentation, they can become lost in the ideas and experiments. It's as if we're experimenting so much that we can forget what was working well in the past.

In the software world, developers have a way of dealing with rapid changes, to prevent becoming lost in the changes. They have a rollback plan, just in case unanticipated problems occur. They can go back to previous versions of the software that were working, essentially undoing the changes they have made.

In golf, we can be mindful of techniques that we have used that have worked well over time. It's like having a rollback plan. We have a set of principles and techniques that we can roll back to if we confuse ourself with our experimentation and learning.

Examine your experimentation and learning approach. Are you changing too fast, too slow, or at the right pace? What's your rollback plan in your short game?

***"I know what has worked for me."***

## October 16: Unconscious Competence

Unconscious competence allows us to execute a swing or stroke without consciously thinking about the swing or stroke. Our mind and body know what to do. To reach unconscious competence, it takes many repetitions physically and imaginatively. Working on a change in technique imaginatively speeds along the learning process to unconscious competence.

Imagine in the near future, chipping and putting, with unconscious competence. Imagine yourself seeing the shot or putt in your mind, feeling the swing or stroke, and then performing the swing or stroke unconsciously. Think of this imaginative practice as being similar to going to the short-game area at your golf course. Practice as many repetitions as you have time to do. There is research that suggests we need repetitions in the thousands before we reach unconscious competence. Continue this mental and physical practice daily until you're able to chip and putt unconsciously.

***"I practice to reach unconscious competence."***

## October 17: Great Lag Putts

The goal of lag putting is to lag within a three-foot circle. Line is important in lag putting, but speed is even more critical. If we don't get the speed right, the line doesn't matter much. The ball won't make it within the desired three-foot circle.

In all parts of our game, the goal is to bring feel—actual physical feelings into our game. In lag putting, it's even more crucial. Practice with different lengths of lag putts and notice the amount of energy required to get the ball within the three-foot circle. When you feel the energy required to make it within the three-foot circle, notice precisely where you feel a sense of energy. It may be in your forearms, or it may be in your shoulders, arms, back, or hands. Notice what part or parts of your body acts as a gauge of energy for your lag putting.

***"I easily lag putts."***

## October 18: Great Short Putts

For those who struggle with putting, the most common struggle is, ironically, the short ones, the ones that should be the easiest. Two things cause golfers to struggle with short putts.

Short putts are hard because the muscle movements are subtle and small, requiring even greater touch than usual. Golfers get off track when they try to guide the ball into the hole by focusing on mechanics rather than feel or target. They try to make a technically perfect stroke, rather than feel the stroke they want.

Short putts become hard when we focus on results. Focusing on results happens when we think about what will happen after the putt. We have such thoughts as, "If I don't make this putt, I will make a bogey." We tend to focus particularly on results with short putts because we expect to make them. This creates internal pressure and tension for many players. With lag putts, we don't typically expect to make them, so they don't normally create high levels of internal pressure and tension for us.

Either approach that focuses on mechanics or a result engages the analytical part of our mind. This creates a break in the otherwise flowing communication between mind and body. It's like trying to have an air traffic controller fly a plane. Give back control in your putting to the pilot in the plane by focusing only on feel, target, and tempo while putting. There's no focus on mechanics or results while putting during a round.

Imagine yourself in your short-game area in your sanctuary, making short putt after short putt. Imagine playing in different situations and different weather conditions, feeling confident over short putts. Imagine your mind being quiet and your emotions being calm. Imagine you have a competitive advantage because of how skilled you're becoming with your short putts.

***"I'm confident and relaxed as I make every short putt."***

## October 19: Performing

Performing when it matters most is an essential skill for competitive golfers, even if the competition is among our regular playing partners. Key situations often show up in the short game. Some golfers naturally like the pressure situations and perform well. Most of us have to learn to enjoy the pressure situations and the opportunity to perform.

There are two essential elements to beginning to perform well when it matters the most. The first essential element is that we have to have a core belief in our ability. If we don't currently feel that we can perform well, then we must believe in our ability to learn to perform well. Learning to perform well in pressure situations in the short game begins with us imagining ourself performing well in pressure situations.

The second essential element is that we need to learn to appreciate and even look forward to performing in meaningful situations. We have to learn to have key moments in rounds elevate us to higher levels of performance. We have to train our thinking, emotions, and physical states to look forward to being in a position during a round when performance matters most. That learning begins in our imagination in our sanctuary.

***"I perform best when it matters the most."***

## October 20: Always Breathing

The short game requires subtle and precise movements. This requires us to manage our physical state closely, more than any other part of the game. Learning to manage our physical state requires practice. Most people don't naturally have the ability to release tension, consciously, from their body. However, we can learn to release tension.

Breathing is a terrific way to manage our physical state. Practice that now by taking a very deep breath, holding it for a few seconds, and then exhaling fully. Notice your physical state. Notice how you can relax, just by breathing deeply and exhaling deeply. Repeat the same exercise. Then repeat it once more.

You can practice breathing and releasing tension on the golf course. It can become part of your pre-shot or pre-putt routine.

***"I release tension by breathing deeply."***

## October 21: Smooth and Rhythmic

Smoothness and rhythm are essential in the short game. There might be some unusual circumstances where we would use an intentionally "jabby" or quick swing with a wedge around the green, but it would be rare. Smooth and rhythmic are the norm around greens. Golfers vary in the speed of their swings and strokes, but the swings and strokes should still be smooth and rhythmical.

We can learn to be smooth and rhythmical with our putting stroke. Feel is once again the key concept for helping us to be smooth and rhythmical. Practice putting different lengths of putts with as smooth and rhythmic a stroke as possible. Notice what physical feelings you have in your body when you do that. The feelings you notice might be in your shoulders, forearms, hands, or any other part of your body that comes to your attention.

Compare the feelings of smooth and rhythmic strokes with strokes that aren't smooth and rhythmic. Notice the physical feelings you have. Perform the same experiment with chips and pitches around the green. Become aware of the feelings of smooth and rhythmic swings versus ones that aren't smooth and rhythmical. The feelings will vary from individual to individual.

***"My putting and chipping are smooth and rhythmical."***

## October 22: Reading Greens

We can use our whole body to read greens. Our body is a very sensitive instrument if we learn to pay attention to it. Our body can feel subtle slopes as we walk across the green.

Similarly, we use our whole mind to read greens. We use our imagination to have a sense of how the ball might roll. We use our analytical ability to remember previous putts, speeds, and slopes.

Imagine that your mind and body are sensitive instruments that can detect even subtle slopes that others can't detect. Imagine becoming an expert green reader. See yourself on your sanctuary movie theater screen and how you move and what you look at when you read greens. You use your imagination effectively while reading greens and putting. Open up all of your senses to reading greens. See if you can notice the overall slope of the golf course. Move your head slightly from side to side and see if the different perspectives don't indicate some subtle slopes. Feel the wind on your skin and whether it's strong enough to influence a putt or chip.

Imagine a ball rolling to the low point on the green. See the grain if there's any. The shiny look on the green tells you the ball is rolling down-grain and will be faster than a ball rolling up-grain. The darker patches tell you the ball is going up-grain and will be slower than the down-grain putts.

***"I see and feel subtle slopes."***

## October 23: Patient Putting

Some days we make great reads and hit great putts, but they just don't go in the hole. That's the nature of putting, particularly on courses where the green conditions are other than Tour caliber. Greens are imperfect. Even a perfectly read and stroked putt may not go in the hole.

We can feel frustrated in a round when putts aren't falling. Frustration is a vicious cycle. Frustration builds frustration, causing tension, which only exacerbates the problems with putting. Rather than becoming frustrated with putts that don't fall in a round, our goal is to make good reads and make good strokes, hitting the putt on line and with the speed we intend. If the putt goes in, that's great. If the putt doesn't go in, we take satisfaction in that we made the best read and stroked the best putt possible. We move on to the next putt.

***"I'm patient with putting."***

## October 24: Trusting Your Stroke

The goal in the short game is to be able to play automatically, without many thoughts, with a focus on feel and targets. Great putters and short-game players are feel players. They may not even be able to tell you exactly what they are doing around the greens. They may have an approach that they can't easily put into words. They use their intuition and their physical feel to decide how to hit a chip or putt.

Find a chipping and putting stroke that feels good to you, is easy to repeat, and hits chips and putts on the line and with the speed that you want most of the time. Find your stroke, particularly the tempo and feel that suits you, and stick with it, perfecting it, feeling it, and letting it become automatic, so that it becomes the foundation of your golf game. We can't trust a stroke that's constantly changing.

***"I trust my chipping and putting stroke."***

## October 25: Great on All Surfaces

If you play competitively, you play on greens with different surfaces. Greens can vary greatly from course to course. Greens can also vary greatly on the same course, from day to day and season to season.

Some golfers allow themselves to dislike certain conditions, such as slow greens or certain types of grasses. By doing so, they reinforce that they expect to perform poorly. In essence, they are creating and reinforcing an excuse to fail prior to playing.

Make the decision today that you'll rise above any conditions on the greens. You affirm that you're mentally strong enough to embrace all conditions and turn that into a competitive advantage. In fact, you're learning to enjoy challenging conditions because it gives you a mental edge against others who don't embrace the reality of the golf course that's in front of them.

***"I embrace all green surfaces and conditions."***

## October 26: Your Private World

Learning to meditate on the golf course is like creating a private world where things are just as we would have them, even when the situation is challenging. A private world is another metaphor for the subconscious mind, similar to the idea of our sanctuary. When chipping and putting, we go into our private world, blocking out everything else that would be a distraction. In the short game, the margin for error is small and requires us to have a high degree of focus.

The more we enter our private world as we meditate, the easier it is to go back repeatedly. With repetition of our meditations in our sanctuary, we begin to take our private world with us to the golf course as we play. Our private world is a perfect place to play golf from and is a formidable competitive advantage, particularly in the short game where focus is paramount.

***"I play from my own private world."***

## October 27: Intuition

The feelings that we have in our body connect to the intuitive part of our mind. We feel something in our body, and we connect with our intuition. Our intuition is central to being a feel player. We can train ourself to use more feel and intuition in our short game.

In your next short-game practice session, work on playing with feel and intuition. You can do that by avoiding the typical analytical and mechanical approaches to golf. When you're chipping, you simply grab a club and hit chips to a target without thinking about how you're going to chip. You can pay attention to your breathing only as you chip.

You can practice in a similar way with your putting. Take your putter and start hitting putts to a target or hole without the usual green reading, practice strokes, and attention to the mechanics of putting. Pay attention to your breathing only as you putt.

***"I play using my intuition."***

## October 28: Mind of a Champion

A champion's mind holds only positive thoughts and images. A champion feels as if she deserves to succeed and deserves to win. A champion feels that she will compete fully. Even if she has not fully mastered her game, she believes she will find a way to win. Champions believe that they will grow into what they already believe about themselves.

Champions use the short game as the foundation of their game. It takes the pressure off all the rest of their game because they believe that they can save strokes by getting up and down from anywhere around the green.

Imagine being a champion of the short game. Imagine your short game being the foundation of your game. Imagine competing to your fullest ability, believing in your ability around the green. Imagine you have the best short game of your competition. Imagine how that would create a positive ripple through your whole game.

***"I'm a short-game champion."***

## October 29: Slow Motion Stroke

If we're working on our short game, we can benefit from practicing putting and chipping strokes in slow motion, doing and feeling exactly what we want. Surely, if we can't make the desired stroke in slow motion, we can't make the stroke and repeat it reliably at regular speed. Our mind and body naturally learn things at slow speeds at first, gradually increasing speeds as we gain competency.

When you practice strokes in slow motion, talk to yourself about what you're doing and what you're feeling. Let your conscious and subconscious mind know exactly what you want to happen.

Be positive and patient with yourself. Treat yourself as a wise and affirming teacher might treat you. Begin to speak to yourself with the voice of a wise and affirming teacher as a regular practice.

***"I feel my chipping and putting strokes in slow motion."***

## October 30: Expectation

If you've ever played with a highly skilled putter or chipper, you expect that player to make a long putt or chip during a round. There's no surprise when that happens. If you watch that golfer's reaction, you'll notice that he or she also expected to make the putt or chip. Often, expectation is what separates a good putter or chipper from an exceptional putter or chipper.

Create the expectation that you're an excellent putter and chipper. You expect to chip balls into the hole even though your goal is to get within 3 feet of the hole. Sometimes good chips go in the hole. You expect to make a long putt or two during a round, even if you're only trying to make a good lag putt. Good lag putts sometimes go in the hole. High expectations precede high performance.

***"I expect to make long chips and putts."***

## October 31: Growing Confidence

Better players create lofty goals for themselves in their short game. They don't just create goals that will allow them to compete against those at their own level. They create goals that will enable them to compete with those at the next level.

What do you need to do to take your short game to the next level? Once you've achieved that goal, how will you feel? What will your confidence level be? That's the confidence level that you should start creating right now. That's the attitude that you should take to your practice sessions. That's the attitude you should take to your rounds on the golf course.

You raise your confidence level by using your imagination. Imagine you're in your sanctuary movie theater watching yourself on the screen sometime in the future. You've become the short-game player you desire to be. Notice how you look, feel, move, and play as you perform around the green. See yourself succeeding and winning. Now imagine you become part of the movie and can see, feel, and experience how it is to be so proficient in your short game.

***"I'm highly confident in my short game."***

# *November: Being a Superb Ball Striker*

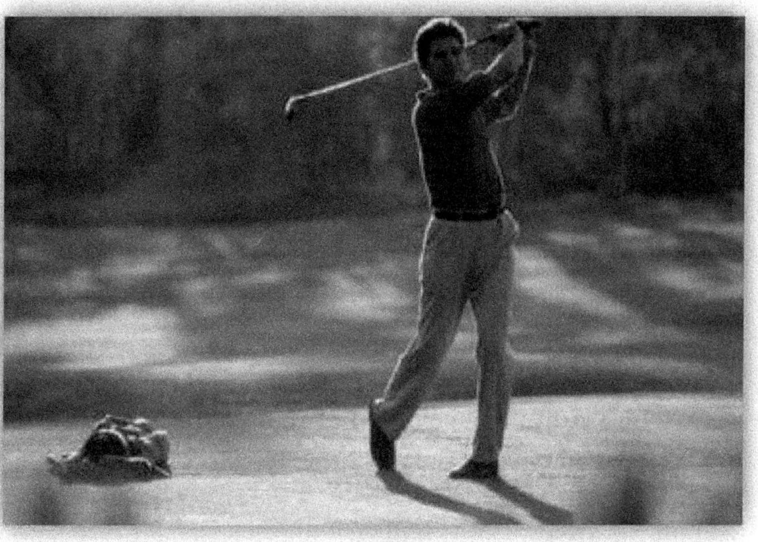

Being a superb ball striker makes golf exceptionally enjoyable. There's a feeling of being in charge of our game, and being able to navigate strategically around a golf course. We can play well, even without being a good ball striker by compensating with a brilliant short game, but it can wear on our psyche and feel as if golf is more about trying to avoid disaster than playing the golf course strategically.

## November 1: What to Improve

Golf is a never-ending game of improvement. Even if we're a talented ball striker, we can still improve.

Complete the following sentences as spontaneously as possible with as many endings as possible. Record your answers for further reflection.

- The clubs that I hit the best are...
- The clubs that I struggle with the most are...
- The shots that I hit the best are...
- The shots that I struggle with the most are...
- The parts of my mental game that help me with ball striking are...
- The parts of my mental game that I struggle with in my ball striking are...
- The things that frustrate me with ball striking are...
- The best parts of my ball striking are...
- The parts of my ball striking that I feel confident in are...
- The parts of my ball striking that I'm least confident in are...
- To be a better ball striker, I need to start...
- To be a better ball striker, I need to stop...

Reflect on the areas of your ball striking that need improvement and imagine practicing and playing in ways that help you to improve. Imagine leveraging your strengths in ball striking more effectively as you manage yourself and the golf courses that you play.

***"I'm improving my ball striking."***

## November 2: Tick Tock

Great ball strikers vary with their tempos. When we watch Tour players, we see that different swing tempos can get the job done well. The key is to find what works for you.

You can learn what tempo works best for you by beginning on the range and experimenting with different tempos. One way to do that is the "tick tock" drill. Begin your backswing by saying the word "tick" to yourself. At impact, say the word "tock" silently in your mind. Experiment with different clubs and different tempos, from fast to slow. Notice what tempo feels good to your body and what produces the most consistent results. If a certain tempo gives consistent results and feels good to your body, you've found the one that works for you. Stick with it until it becomes unconscious competence.

***"I swing at a tempo that's right for me."***

## November 3: Slow Motion Practice

If we can't do something in slow motion, we almost certainly can't do it at full speed. Become acquainted with your golf swing in slow motion. Know what you want your body to do and how it feels to do it.

As you're making slow motion swings, narrate to yourself what your body is doing and what sensations you're feeling. This is a powerful way of owning your golf swing. It will take some time and practice for you to become deeply aware of how your bodily movements feel and then to develop a language to describe the various sensations.

***"I practice my swing in slow motion."***

## November 4: In the Middle

In terms of ball striking, we know we're on the right path when we're consistently hitting the ball in the middle of the clubface.

If you've ever been to a PGA Tour or LPGA Tour event in windy conditions, you'll see how little the wind affects their ball. That's because they consistently hit the ball in the middle of the clubface. Hitting the ball in the middle of the clubface decreases sidespin and produces consistent yardages with each club.

Make the decision today to have a goal of always hitting the ball in the middle of the clubface. Make that the focus of your ball striking practice. Shaping shots can come after that.

***"I hit the ball in the middle of the clubface."***

## November 5: Sense of Timing

Some insights we have about our golf swing can have a sense of timing with them. Some insights take years to unfold and become fully relevant to us. Sometimes we need time and experience to add other pieces to the puzzle first before the knowledge we have is useful to us. Sometimes things we have learned in the past come around again for us to relearn. We need to be patient with our learning, perhaps keeping a journal of insights we learn along the way to finding our own swing.

***"I'm patient with learning."***

## November 6: Being Athletic

Some people allow themselves to believe they aren't athletic because they compare themselves to prototypical athletes. The faulty assumption here is that there's only one correct model of being athletic. There are many kinds of athletic. There's athleticism in balance, speed, strength, timing, power, fine movements, feel, touch for delicate shots, and the ability of our body to do what we want. Being a good ball striker is an excellent demonstration of athleticism. Appreciate the unique ways that you're athletic. Appreciate how good you are right now and how good you are becoming.

***"I'm athletic and hit great shots."***

## November 7: Learning Builds on Itself

Learning isn't like adding a piece after piece to a large, complex puzzle. Learning is more like having one piece of the puzzle that fits in the middle of many other pieces, making sense of a number of different pieces. The more we know, the more we can know.

When we learn a system of swinging the club from one skillful teacher, we create the possibility of efficient learning, where we have many pieces of the puzzle that go together and make sense of each other. When we choose little bits of knowledge about a swing from many disparate sources, we may be trying to assemble a puzzle that won't fit together.

Decide today to be a better student of your swing. Find someone who has a swing that you admire and that you think fits your physique and athletic ability. Learn that swing and way of playing golf. Learn from a master and see how you can use the approach and make it your own. Then stick with it.

***"I learn efficiently."***

## November 8: Knowing Your Strengths

Sometimes we can create problems for ourself when we become too focused on fixing what we think is wrong with our golf game. Sometimes the best approach is to focus even more intently on what we do well and see if we can create leverage with that. For example, if we have an average distance off the tee with a driver, the best use of our time and energy may not be to try to increase our length off the tee. It may turn out that we're an exceptional wedge player and can create leverage in our game by becoming even better at our wedge play.

Complete the following sentences as spontaneously as possible with as many endings as possible. Record your answers for further reflection.

- The tee shots that I like the most are...
- The shots that I like the most are...
- My favorite designs of golf holes are...
- My favorite clubs are...
- The most fun shots for me are...
- The best parts of my game are...
- The shots that I feel the most confident with are...
- The parts of my ball striking that I like the most are...
- The parts of golf that I believe I can become highly skilled at are...

Imagine you're playing to your strengths in the near and distant future. Imagine you're practicing to improve your strengths even more, creating leverage in your golf game to play at a higher level.

***"I build on my strengths."***

## November 9: Playing With Energy

Golf is a whole lot of fun if we're playing with imagination versus fighting our swing and obsessing with mechanical swing thoughts. We can play golf either analytically or imaginatively. Analysis takes energy. Playing imaginatively provides energy. Imagining the swings you want, feeling the swings, and focusing on targets all provide energy. Obsessing about our score, focusing on past shots, focusing on future shots, and tweaking swing mechanics during a round all take energy.

If you are finding yourself exhausted after playing, you may be going about it in a way that's not allowing you to be your best. Notice what gives you energy. Then practice and play that way.

***"I play golf with energy."***

## November 10: Being Unique

Reflect for a few minutes on how your approach to golf is different from people you've played with over the years. What's unique about your body, your swing, your thinking, your decision-making, your emotions on the golf course, and the way that you interact with others?

Take some time in your sanctuary to explore the things that you've done over the years that you believe have helped you become a better ball striker. As you think about how you're unique and what you've done over the years, what might you try to be a better ball striker, now and in the future?

***"I know what works for me."***

## November 11: Superior Ball Striking

Being a superior ball striker makes golf a lot more fun unless we crave the adrenalin rush of hitting shots from trees and other "interesting" places. Hitting the ball all over the golf course turns golf into a game of survival.

We begin the journey to becoming a superior ball striker by making the decision to be a superior ball striker. Go to your sanctuary movie theater and watch movies of yourself in the future being a superior ball striker. Imagine seeing yourself from the time you decided to be a superior ball striker to the time you became a superior ball striker. Notice how you practice, how you play, and how you work on your mental game. Now become part of the movie and notice how you feel and carry yourself, and how you think about ball striking.

***"I'm becoming a superior ball striker."***

## November 12: Feel Player

A focus on mechanics and mechanical swing thoughts can get us only so far because of the nature of mechanical thinking. High-level athletic performance is primarily an imaginative activity as opposed to an analytical one. In addition, our bodies change subtly every day, particularly as we get older. When we play mechanically, we may not be paying attention to subtle changes in our body.

A golf swing is a concrete thing. A physical feeling bridges the gap between a mechanical swing thought and a golf swing. Become a student of what your body is doing based on how it feels when you swing a club. To become a feel player is to be intimately aware of bodily sensations as we swing. We must be able to swing with a feeling in mind while being able to hit the ball to different targets.

***"I rely on feel in my golf swing."***

## November 13: Playing Artfully

To be free to play golf and not play "golf swing," we have to learn to stop trying to control things that we can't fully control. At its core, an obsession with mechanics is a desire to overcontrol our golf swing. For those of us who have perfectionist tendencies, it's a seductive approach to playing golf. The seductive idea is that if we can create the perfect golf swing, we will have a perfect golf game. Golf just doesn't work that way. Mechanics are important in the learning process, but at some point, we have to set them aside and go play golf artfully. There's no such thing as the "perfect swing." Notice how many great golfers swing the club differently.

***"I play golf artfully."***

## November 14: Learning on the Range

When we go to the range, we should practice hitting different shots as opposed to what many of us do, which is to work on our golf swing. Focusing on hitting shots turns range time into learning how to play golf creatively, intuitively, and with the proper feel.

At a minimum, schedule times on the range where you work on shot making only and not mechanics. Spend time hitting the ball to targets without any mechanical thoughts. Being a great ball striker is about hitting shots to clear targets with a quiet mind.

***"I hit the ball to clear targets."***

## November 15: Hitting the Ball Squarely

Learning to hit the ball the way we want involves both bodily movement and our mind, particularly our imagination. The first step towards physically doing anything is to imagine ourself doing it. Our subconscious mind doesn't distinguish between what we imagine and what we experience. When we imagine ourself doing something, our subconscious believes it's a real experience. We see this phenomenon most clearly with our dreams, which show us how our subconscious mind works. When we're dreaming, the dreams are real. Even when we wake up, our dreams still feel like a vivid and real experience. Subconscious thinking is an "experience." The more we imagine ourself doing something, the more we experience it.

Based on this understanding, we can mentally practice physical movements. We can practice our ball striking by imagining ourself hitting balls squarely in the middle of the clubface.

Imagine a bull's-eye in the middle of every club in your bag. Imagine hitting balls to targets. Every ball you hit, you hit right in the middle of the clubface with the club squared up just the way you want. Imagine how it feels in your body as you're hitting balls in the middle of the clubface. The more balls you hit in your imagination, the more you experience yourself becoming a better ball striker.

***"I use my imagination to practice ball striking."***

## November 16: Imaginative Pre-Shot Routine

Pre-shot routines allow us to play golf without unduly engaging our analytical ability. Our analytical ability is necessary and wonderful, but when we overuse it, it's the enemy of talented ball striking and playing in the zone. We want to have a pre-shot routine that's more imaginative than analytical.

Imagine being on your sanctuary golf course, playing a round of golf. For each shot, you go through your pre-shot routine. You imagine your target, where you want to hit the ball. You imagine the exact swing that will produce the shot. You imagine feeling what your body is doing in your practice swing. You imagine stepping up and hitting the shot to your target, having only the target filling your mind.

Imagine yourself going through your pre-shot routine and hitting many wonderful shots on your sanctuary golf course. Imagine how good it feels to have such a simple and powerful pre-shot routine. Imagine yourself in tournaments, staying with the same pre-shot routine, performing superbly, just the way you want.

***"I have an imaginative pre-shot routine."***

## November 17: Connecting Feel

Being conscious of the feelings that we have in our body when we make a good swing takes some development for most of us. Sometimes there aren't adequate words to describe what we feel, but we're still aware of the feelings.

Simply having an awareness of our desired feelings in a golf swing isn't sufficient for great ball striking. We have to be able to connect our feeling of a good swing to the target where we want the ball to go. A great-feeling swing connecting in our mind to an ill-defined target creates inconsistent results. A great-feeling swing connecting to a vivid target creates consistent golf shots.

We can practice swing feelings connected to targets effectively on the range. Make that a normal part of your practice. Learn to recognize a great-feeling swing that hits the ball to your targets. That's the key to becoming not simply a good ball striker, but a fantastic ball striker.

***"I feel my swing connecting to my target."***

## November 18: Trusting Your Mind

Our mind communicates subconsciously with our body, telling it what to do to give us the results that we want. If we try to micromanage how our mind communicates with our body, we limit the ability of our subconscious mind to have our body move athletically. It's like an overbearing boss micromanaging an employee. It stifles creativity and natural ability.

Try practicing your golf swing by focusing on the result that you want, not how you want your body to do it. On the range, keep swinging to a target until your body moves naturally. Your mind knows what to do. Your body knows what to do. Just trust them to do what you want.

Practice trusting your mind and body connection. As you practice, use an affirmation to reinforce what you're learning. Before you make each swing with your club, say something such as, "*I trust my mind and body to swing to my target.*"

***"I trust my mind and body to swing to my target."***

## November 19: Joyful Ball Striking

Go to your practice range in your sanctuary where you can imagine practicing your ball striking. Imagine practicing your ball striking with joy. Imagine how that feels in every part of your body as you practice with joy. Imagine practicing in slow motion and feeling great joy. Imagine what parts of your body feel the sensation of joy. How would you describe that feeling to others? Imagine practicing in fast motion and feeling great joy. In what parts of your body would you feel joy physically? How would you describe that feeling to others?

***"I feel joy as I practice my ball striking."***

## November 20: Experimenting With Athleticism

Try a little experiment next time you're on the golf course practicing. Find a steep sidehill lie and pick out a target. Take a couple of practice swings without trying to tell your body how you want to swing. Just take some easy, slow swings and notice how your body is reacting and moving in response to a challenging situation. Perhaps you can trust your athletic ability more than you have in the past.

***"I trust my athletic ability."***

## November 21: Repeatable Swing

There's no swing on earth that repeats exactly every time. That's part of being human. Our body changes a little bit every day. However, our goal is to have as repeatable a swing as possible. Our goal should be to find a swing that's as natural, simple, and athletic as possible. There are four components to having a repeatable swing.

One, we have a mental image of our swing. Seeing ourself on video or in a mirror can help us understand what we're doing objectively. Sometimes what we feel we're doing and what we're actually doing is different.

Two, we have to be able to recognize the physical sensations or feelings that come from making a good swing.

Three, we have to understand a few key positions that our body and club go through in order to ensure that we're making the same swings. If unchecked, our swing usually changes incrementally over time.

Four, our swing has to fit our body and age. There's no point in trying to swing like Ben Hogan if our body simply can't perform that swing.

***"I have a repeatable and effective swing."***

## November 22: Target Focus

Moe Norman, one of the great ball strikers, was laser focused on targets with every shot. During the swing, he held an image of the target in his mind and swung the club to the target. He didn't hold mechanical types of swing thoughts in his mind during the swing. This allowed him to be athletic and fluid while using his imagination to the fullest in his golf swing. Even when he was on the range hitting balls, Norman would imagine he was playing golf holes and hitting shots based on his memory of playing.

***"I hit the ball to targets."***

## November 23: Connecting Mind and Body

Being a skilled ball striker requires that our mind and body work well together. When we play in the zone, our mind and body connect effortlessly and efficiently. The golf swing is too complex a motion to manage consciously. When players become overly conscious of their swings, they become mechanical and limit their ability to perform at their highest levels.

Explore the ideas you have about the connection between your mind and body by completing the following sentences as spontaneously as possible with as many endings as possible. Record your answers for further reflection.

- The connections between my mind and body are...
- Sometimes when I'm hitting shots, my body feels...
- Sometimes when I'm hitting shots, my mind is...
- When I'm hitting balls, my mind and body are...
- I feel as if my mind and body are...
- I think I could be a better ball striker if my mind and body were...
- The things I need to improve about my mind and body connection are...
- The things I don't understand about my mind and body connection are...

We want to feel as if our mind and body connect effortlessly. We want to feel that they move together like two dancers in perfect harmony. We use our imagination to tell our mind and body what we want to accomplish. Imagine you're playing effortlessly. Your mind and body are doing precisely what you want.

***"My mind and body connect effortlessly."***

## November 24: Learning From Others

It's good to learn to trust our insights and decisions about how to improve our game. However, there's a balance between learning from our own experiences and learning from others.

We build trust with others on a foundation of respect for an individual's uniqueness. Find a coach who understands you.

Seek out a coach who has many ways to teach, who begins teaching you by getting to know you and how you approach golf. Who can you trust to teach you about ball striking?

***"I trust others to help me along my journey."***

## November 25: Noticing Improvements

There are different kinds of improvements that we can make that may well affect the quality of our ball striking. Sometimes we're improving at golf but fail to recognize it because we're not looking in all of the places where we might improve. Consider the following:

- We improve the feel of our shots.
- We improve the quality of our results.
- We improve our mental attitude about what we're doing.
- We improve statistically in various parts of our game, such as driving distance, driving accuracy, greens-in-regulation, and proximity to the pin.
- We improve how we flight the ball and shape shots.
- We improve the consistency of our swings.
- We improve our mental approach to hitting great shots.

In what other ways might you improve your ball striking?

***"I notice improvements that can make a great difference."***

## November 26: Our Clubs

As long as we view our clubs as something other than an extension of our body, arms, hands, and fingers, we may have a tendency to do things with the clubs that are unnatural. Injuries and inconsistency occur when we treat the club as something other than a natural extension of our body. Placing a golf club in our hands doesn't somehow make unnatural movements desirable. Find a golf swing that feels natural to your body, and your clubs will start to feel like a natural extension of your body.

***"My clubs are an extension of my body."***

## November 27: Feel Your Swing

We need to convert swing thoughts into swing feelings to be effective and make the right connection between our mind and body. Pay attention to what you feel in your body as you swing your clubs. Learn to recognize the feelings of you making solid swings. Pay attention to where you're feeling sensations in your body. Be specific about where you're feeling sensations. If you feel a sensation in your arms, where specifically in your arms do you feel something?

***"I feel my swing."***

## November 28: Lust for Technology

Technology in golf can make a difference in our game, for sure. However, some of us lust for the latest technology, believing that we have to have the latest and best technology. Technology can become a substitute for purposeful practice and solid technique.

Ironically, when technology becomes essential to us, it starts to erode confidence in our own athletic ability. Technology becomes a substitute for confidence. The point is to use technology, but don't be used by it. Be selective. Trust your skill. Believe in yourself, your practice, and your ball striking ability so much that you imagine that you could play with old technology and still be great. That places confidence in the right place, which is your ability.

***"I use technology in ways that work for me."***

## November 29: Making Good Decisions

Being a good ball striker depends in part on making good decisions on the golf course, knowing what shot to hit with what club. To be able to know how a good decision feels, we have to pay attention to our decisions, and we have to understand what makes a good decision.

Complete the following sentences as spontaneously as possible with as many endings as possible. Record your answers for further reflection.

- Some of the best decisions I have made on the golf course are...
- The decisions that typically get me in trouble on the golf course are...
- When choosing a club to hit, I know I'm making good decisions when...
- When deciding what shots to hit, I know I'm making good decisions when...
- I usually know when I'm making good decisions on the golf course when...
- I usually know when I'm making bad decisions on the golf course when...
- When I make good decisions on the golf course, I feel...
- When I make bad decisions on the golf course, I feel...

Reflect on your answers and notice the ones that have the most energy or surprise you the most. Imagine you're making the right decisions on the golf course in the near and distant future. Imagine you're a solid strategist on the golf course, always choosing the right clubs and the right swings to hit your ball to your targets.

***"I make great decisions on the golf course."***

## November 30: Lust for Power

The lust for power and more distance can ruin golf games and golf swings at all levels. There are two reasons for this. One, there's a natural limit to what an individual can do physically. The lust for power can push us to exceed what we can do naturally with a golf club. When our swing becomes unnatural, inconsistency and injuries are the most likely results. Two, when we lust for power and that becomes the central focus of our practice and workouts, we tend to ignore the other parts of our game, which require finesse and equal amounts of practice.

One great way of testing whether you're trying to do something unnatural with your body is to notice if you're creating tension in your body because of what you're trying to do. Tension creates injuries. Tension kills speed and athleticism.

Test for yourself. Swing a driver as fast as you can without creating tension anywhere in your body. Notice how it feels when you swing without tension. Become familiar with what causes tension and what keeps athleticism in your golf swing.

***"I use my power artfully."***

# *December: Being Mentally Tough*

To be a great champion is to be mentally tough. To be mentally tough requires us to accept that golf competitions are as much a mental test as they are a physical test. Being mentally tough is making good decisions in the heat of competition and doing the things that the rest of the field is unwilling or unable to do. Mental toughness begins by believing that we can handle anything or learn to handle anything.

## December 1: Mental Toughness

Mental toughness means different things to different people. To understand what it means to you, complete the following sentences as spontaneously as possible with as many endings as possible. Record your answers for further reflection.

- I think I have been the most mentally tough in golf when...
- I think I have been the most mentally tough in life when...
- I think mental toughness is different for me because...
- In the future, I will be mentally tougher when...
- I think I could learn to be mentally tougher by...
- The things I don't know about mental toughness are...
- To be mentally tougher, I need to start...
- To be mentally tougher, I need to stop...

***"I understand mental toughness."***

## December 2: Being Mentally Tough

Mental toughness means that we do everything within our power to perform our best. Mental toughness is a skill that we can learn, but it may require that we develop some new "mental muscles." Some of us have loads of talent but fall short of where we should be. We undercut our ability subconsciously. Deep inside our sanctuary, we don't fully believe in our ability and haven't worked to develop that belief in the right ways.

The key to changing subconscious structures of thought requires that we communicate with ourself at the level of our sanctuary. We learn to communicate effectively with our subconscious mind by daily meditations.

***"I'm mentally tough."***

## December 3: Deciding

A few lucky people seem to be naturally, mentally tough competitors. For most of us, we have to learn to be mentally tough. For those of us who aren't naturally mentally tough, we have to understand the need for it, decide to be mentally tough, and then take action.

From your sanctuary, remember as many positive decisions as you can that you've made in life and golf. Some great decisions can be decisions not to do something. Remember how it felt emotionally and physically to make a great decision. Have those feelings magnify and intensify as if you could turn up the intensity dial on the great feelings. Now imagine accepting the challenge and feeling confident about being a mentally tough golfer with those same feelings and intensity.

***"I have decided to be mentally tough."***

## December 4: Feeling Mental Toughness

In your sanctuary, reflect on the times when you were mentally tough—in golf, other sports, and life in general. When you do, pay attention to how it felt emotionally and physically. Notice how things might have looked to you then. Imagine what you might have been thinking at that time. As much as you can, experience the same sensations that you felt on those occasions. When you've remembered a number of experiences, imagine you're bringing those same feelings, insights, and physical sensations to your current golf game. Imagine you're playing with the same or even higher levels of mental toughness.

***"I feel mentally tough."***

## December 5: Power and Self-Acceptance

Mentally tough people are powerful people. They think and act in ways that others don't. Powerful people accept who they are and use their power. They aren't afraid of being powerful. Being powerful doesn't necessarily mean that we have a lot of money or other resources. Being powerful is more about being who we decide to be in life. People who live without their power criticize themselves for their past and accept the negative perceptions of others.

We can't change the past. Everyone has made mistakes, but powerful people let go of what holds them back. Powerful people view the past as "data." They use it to help guide them in the present and future. Every one of us can decide not to use the data of the past to tear ourself down, but to use that data to help guide us in the present and future. That process can begin today with a decision to use the data of the past for our own benefit, and not be used by the data of the past.

Golf and life connect with each other. We are in golf as we are in life. Golf is a perfect opportunity to learn and practice self-acceptance. Whatever mistakes we have made in the past are simply data for the present and future. Golf is about being present to our power to play skillfully today.

***"I'm powerful."***

## December 6: An Unfolding Story

The big moments in golf, both the positive and negative ones, give us a snapshot of whether we're progressing towards our aspirations. Sometimes we sense we're making progress towards our goals and sometimes we sense we're falling short.

However, those snapshots aren't necessarily the best way to sense whether we're moving in the direction we want. We can play golf for a lifetime if we're healthy. Sometimes there are plateaus and valleys in golf. It's easy to feel encouraged when things are going just the way we want. However, in the plateaus and valleys, we need to remember that we're an unfolding story with many chapters and that we require patience and persistence to succeed. Even if our dreams take a lifetime to fulfill, we want to keep moving ahead, even when the next mountaintop is not in view. That's the essence of mental toughness.

***"I keep going."***

## December 7: Challenges

Deep inside, if we believe that what lies before us is insurmountable, then we will start making excuses and subconsciously look for ways to fail. We're planning to fail. Excuses are red flags that point to a lack of clear and consistent belief, deep inside.

When we're mentally tough, we don't see any challenges as insurmountable. We see challenges as invitations. They are invitations to rise to new levels of performance and to learn from the challenges, whether they go as we hope or don't. Either way the experiences can be positive. We learn from everything we do and seek to find a path forward.

***"I willingly accept challenges."***

## December 8: Images of Mental Toughness

Imagine you're in your sanctuary movie theater watching movies of yourself and others playing and competing with mental toughness. The images can be of golf or any other sport. Imagine your sports heroes playing with mental toughness. How does that look? What are the images that stand out in your imagination? Now have the images become even bigger, brighter, and more vivid, with clear and pleasing sound effects. Notice what colors and sounds stand out to you. Have them fill the screen and your imagination.

Now imagine being in the movie, playing golf in the future with the same intensity, feeling, and clarity that you're feeling right now.

***"I see and feel myself being mentally tough."***

## December 9: Passion

Great champions know where they want to go and what they want to do. They execute a plan. Inevitably they say, "No, thank you" to many things in life that aren't going to get them where they want to be. They have to practice, take care of themselves, and take care of their responsibilities outside of sports.

Self-control isn't primarily about exerting willpower. It's more about having a deep passion for what we're trying to accomplish. Passion is a fire burning inside that gets us up in the morning and propels us through the day, inspiring us to do the tasks that lead to success.

In your sanctuary, find your passion for what you want to accomplish. Grow your passion and use it to propel you toward what you want in golf.

***"I deeply connect to my passion for golf."***

## December 10: Defining Moments

Champions can always tell us the points in their careers that were defining moments—when they stepped up their game and made enormous strides towards being the athlete they were dreaming of being. A defining moment is like a graduation ceremony where we experience a pivotal transition that propels us forward, never to return to the same level. Sometimes it takes some time to pass before we realize that we have experienced a defining moment. We don't understand every defining moment at the time.

What have been your defining moments in golf so far? Let your imagination go and dream of your future as a golfer and how it might be to experience some more defining moments. Begin to prepare for the next stage in your golfing journey, even before you arrive at the next stage.

***"I appreciate defining moments."***

## December 11: Conversations

Go to a place in your sanctuary, where you're at peace and connect with your deeper self. Take some time to recognize people in life and sports who have demonstrated mental toughness from your perspective. They can be living, passed on, or even imaginary people, such as characters in movies. Imagine that you sit in the middle of as many mentally tough people as you can imagine. You can ask them anything about mental toughness. They can ask you anything. You might pose some questions such as the following.

- How did you develop mental toughness?
- What's mental toughness from your perspective?
- What are some keys to being mentally tough when we feel in over our heads?
- How is mental toughness different in sports and life?
- What got you through your toughest times in sports?
- How can I development toughness?
- How will I know I'm mentally tough?

***"I recognize mental toughness."***

## December 12: Confident Places

Mentally tough golfers are confident golfers. Go to a place in your sanctuary where you feel confident. The place may be somewhere that you remember being confident in the past. The place may be an imaginary place. The place may be somewhere that you imagine yourself to be in the future.

When you're in that place of confidence, what do you feel, emotionally and physically? When you're in that place, how do you think? What do you do in that place? Imagine that when you're in your place of confidence, something unexpected happens. How do you deal with unexpected events when you're in your place of confidence? How do you feel about other people? How do you feel about yourself as a golfer?

Imagine going to another place of confidence in your sanctuary. Experience how it feels and how you think in that place. What do you do in that place? How do you deal with unexpected events in that place? How do you feel about other people? How do you feel about yourself a golfer?

***"I have places of confidence."***

## December 13: Present to the Moment

Mental toughness requires concentration. The concentration required in competition is a complete focus on the present moment, focusing on what we require at the moment. It takes mental toughness to discipline our thinking to the present moment. If we're between shots, then it's time to be present to walking, relaxing, conversing with playing partners, and enjoying the moment. If we're getting ready to hit our next shot or putt, then we're giving ourself physically, emotionally, and imaginatively to what we must do in order to succeed.

***"I give myself completely to the present moment."***

## December 14: Acknowledge and Let Go

Mental toughness is a disciplined way of thinking and feeling. Not everything that happens in a round of golf is going to be what we want. Things happen. We hit good shots and poor shots. We have good breaks and bad breaks. Mentally tough competitors have the ability to acknowledge what has happened and then let go.

Acknowledging that something didn't happen as we wanted is a way of letting off steam, of dealing with disappointment in the moment, rather than trying to ignore it and let it build up. Find a routine for acknowledging and letting go. Perhaps your routine might be simply saying, "That didn't go the way I wanted." Then take a deep breath and say, "Time to move on." Experiment with your own routine for acknowledging and letting go. Routines that involve deep breathing are typically the most powerful because they relax our mind and our body.

***"I acknowledge what happens and let go."***

## December 15: Streams of Confidence

Confidence is easy when things are going well. Mentally tough competitors find a way to be confident, even in trying moments when others would be discouraged.

You have access to unlimited streams of confidence. Your imagination is the doorway to those streams of confidence. Even in the most challenging times, you can imagine you're coming out of the gloom into the golden light of your hopes and dreams.

In your sanctuary, remember when you came through tough times and how it felt to come through them. Remember what you were thinking that helped you believe you would come through them. Remember how it felt to believe in yourself when others might have doubted you. Imagine how you will use tough times in the future to build your confidence.

***"I have streams of confidence."***

## December 16: Internal Barriers

Mentally tough competitors are constantly challenging internal barriers to their success. Everyone has internal barriers to their success. Some don't recognize that they have barriers. Some feel them to be impassable. Mentally tough golfers are aware of them and feel them to be temporary.

The first step toward overcoming barriers is to recognize them and become conscious of what they are. The second step is to realize that we can overcome all internal barriers. A common barrier many golfers face is the inability to shoot low scores and have career-best rounds. For example, some golfers struggle to shoot lower than 100, others 90, 80, and 70.

Complete the following sentences as spontaneously as possible with as many endings as possible. Record your answers for further reflection.

- I could be a tougher competitor in golf if...
- The things that most frustrate me with golf are...
- If I could change some things to help me be mentally tougher, I would...
- Internally, I don't always believe in my mental toughness because...
- The things that always seem to get me down are...
- The things holding me back from being my best are...
- When I have a chance to shoot low rounds, I usually...
- To get past my internal barriers, I need to start...
- To get past my internal barriers, I need to stop...

If you found there are barriers keeping you from being your best, acknowledge them and let them go. Imagine in the near future, playing superb golf without the internal barriers that have been holding you back.

***"I challenge my internal barriers."***

## December 17: Disciplined Thinking

Being mentally tough requires disciplined thinking. We have to decide when it's time to be analytical and when it's time to be imaginative. Both analytical and imaginative thinking are keys to performing our best.

Analytical thinking is good for gathering facts and weighing options. When we're considering what shot to hit, how environmental factors might affect the ball, and what risk factors there are, then analytical thinking is essential.

Imagination is best when we're going through our pre-shot routine, or working with internal resources, such as confidence, resilience, and summoning the energy to make a birdie and finish a tournament.

***"I fully use my mind to win."***

## December 18: Difficult Conditions

Being able to play well in difficult conditions is no accident. We have to prepare mentally and physically to compete in difficult conditions. We build mental toughness in our training. We can simulate playing in difficult conditions as much as possible. We can learn from elite military units who train in ways that are as realistic and challenging as possible. Going to the range to practice when conditions are perfect develops our ability to play in perfect conditions. Practicing in difficult conditions prepares us mentally and physically to be able to play great when we feel the most challenged. If we can play in difficult conditions, we can play in perfect conditions.

For mental practice, imagine you're playing superbly and truly enjoying playing in all sorts of difficult conditions. Imagine you're playing well in windy, cold, rainy, hot, and hilly conditions. Imagine feeling mentally tough and enjoying that feeling more than ever.

Play well in your imagination, and it will translate to the golf course. Imagine you have a competitive edge because of how you've prepared yourself mentally and physically. You're always mentally tough.

***"I play well in all conditions."***

## December 19: Helpful Motivation

Mentally tough golfers motivate themselves. Sometimes they motivate themselves by positive experiences. Sometimes they motivate themselves by negative experiences. Both sources of motivation can be useful as long as they empower us to grow and move forward in healthy ways.

Motivations aren't helpful when they prevent us from developing and empowering ourself. For example, we can be highly motivated to avoid being in situations that have the risk of failure or embarrassment. If we choose to hold on to this form of motivation, we limit what we're willing to do to develop ourself and move forward. Helpful motivations are open to challenges that bring new experiences and growth. Whether we're successful in what we do or not, we use the experiences to learn, grow, make adjustments, and succeed in the end.

***"I focus on helpful motivations."***

## December 20: Enjoying the Moment

Mental toughness doesn't mean that we're always tough-minded as if we were a car that had only one gear. We know when it's time to switch into competitive mode and when to switch it off. Being in a competitive mode is a highly focused and often intense state of mind. Mental toughness is a disciplined mind that does what we want when we want it. There's a time to be competitive and intense and time to relax.

Much of life is good, simple moments—moments that may not have much lasting import, but they are moments that are worth appreciating nonetheless. Much of golf, too, is good, simple moments—the time between shots, enjoying some pleasant banter, and enjoying being in a beautiful place. It's our awareness of the simple moments and appreciation of them that makes them come alive for us and makes life and golf much richer than they would be without the awareness. Mentally tough players know when to be tough and when to relax.

***"I enjoy the simple moments of playing golf."***

## December 21: Mentally Tough Memories

Mentally tough golfers have selective memories. They remember what they want to remember, even if it's purely a subconscious process.

Some golfers subconsciously assign more importance to their negative or sad memories. Mentally tough golfers subconsciously assign more importance to the positive memories. They don't weigh down their consciousness with a catalog of failures. They don't come to a tournament or match remembering failures. They expect to play well and compete with all of their ability.

We can reinforce our positive memories by meditating on them regularly in our sanctuary movie theater and making the memories brighter, more vivid, more intense, and more memorable in pleasant and powerful ways.

***"I remember my successes in golf."***

## December 22: Playing

Mentally tough golfers keep golf in perspective. Golf can become frustrating if we make it more than it is. Golf is a game. Even for professional golfers, if they make golf the most prominent focus in their life, it can become a monster. When golf becomes something other than a game, it becomes either more about Ego or it becomes work. When we don't "play golf," we engage the wrong parts of our mind. When we play golf for the pure joy of playing, there's a lightness and effortlessness about it. Playing golf to feed an Ego or for work can turn golf into something that leaves us feeling drained.

There's a reason that we call golf a game. Even if we play golf professionally, we still play it best as a game. Anything that we do "as a job" can be devoid of passion. Ideally, even our livelihood should be something that we love to do, that doesn't feel like work and that engages our passion and feels meaningful. That feeds our spirit.

***"I play for the pure joy of playing."***

## December 23: Joy in Competition

Some of us find that playing with good golfers causes us to feel nervous. Sometimes that's helpful and sometimes not. It's helpful if it motivates us to play better. It's unhelpful if it creates tension and poor decision-making. If we feel tension, often all we need to do is to train our mind and emotions to be happy for the opportunity to perform against some good competition.

Imagine being in tournaments in the near and distant future, playing against high levels of competition. Imagine you're feeling loose, relaxed, and appreciative for the opportunity to compete. As the competitions become increasingly skillful, imagine you rise to the level of the competition, becoming even more joyful, relaxed, skillful, and confident.

***"I rise to the level of competition."***

## December 24: Defining Success

Golf is a tough game to win. Even the greatest players win only a fraction of the events they play. Mentally tough golfers appreciate the success that they have, even when they do not win. It's like always keeping gas in the tank for the journey. We learn to celebrate not only winning, but also many different aspects of succeeding in golf.

Complete the following sentences as spontaneously as possible with as many endings as possible. Record your answers for further reflection.

- The things I most appreciate about what I have accomplished in golf are...
- I'm most proud of myself in golf when...
- Even when I don't win, I can celebrate...
- I feel the most successful in golf when...
- I think some of my greatest successes have been...
- I can share my success with others by...
- For me, success is different from others because...
- At the end of my playing days, if there's an end, I will be most happy with...
- I think success in golf in the future for me is...

***"I decide what success means."***

## December 25: Celebrating Successes

Successes in golf are like having money in the bank when we need it. Mentally tough golfers focus on keeping their perspective about what they are accomplishing.

Create a ritual around your successes to make them even more memorable. Find a way to give those you care about and yourself a reward for your successes. Share your successes with those around you who have helped you achieve your goals. Create milestones for yourself, things that are necessary for you to accomplish in your golf game, and establish different rewards to make each of them more memorable. Perhaps you can start a ritual of taking a loved one or close friend to a celebration dinner when you achieve a positive result in a tournament.

***"I celebrate successes."***

## December 26: Always Learning

Mentally tough golfers are constantly learning. One of the best ways to eliminate anger, frustration, and disappointment in our golf game is to accept that golf comes with many opportunities for learning. Anger, frustration, and disappointment in golf come from perfectionist tendencies. We expect ourself to perform closer to our ideal. If we miss our mark, anger, frustration, and disappointment can take up too much space in our mind. Even in a great round, we will make mistakes. Accept that and you'll be on the way to more productive and joyful golf.

***"I'm always learning."***

## December 27: Competing Fully

Mentally tough players don't make excuses, but compete fully, with no reservation, every time they play. Everyone feels aches and pains and has good and bad days mentally, emotionally, and physically. Mentally tough players, play through challenging circumstances, not fighting them or making that bigger than they are, but working through them in the best ways possible.

Complete the following sentences as spontaneously as possible with as many endings as possible. Record your answers for further reflection.

- To me, competing fully means...
- The keys to competing fully for me are...
- I would compete fully more often if...
- In the past, I have not competed fully because...
- The things holding me back from competing fully are...
- To compete fully more often, I need to start...
- To compete fully more often, I need to stop...

If you found there are things keeping you from competing fully, acknowledge them and let them go, imagining yourself being able to compete fully every time you tee it up.

***"I compete fully."***

## December 28: Remembering to Breathe

When athletes become nervous, they tend to shallow their breathing or hyperventilate. Both states, oxygen-starved or hyperventilated, place athletes in a position to perform below their capability.

It sounds easy, but obvious, when we think about it. Part of being a mentally tough golfer is remembering to make deep, regular breathing a part of our practice and competitions. Make it part of your pre-shot and pre-putt routines. Take one or two deep breaths. Get in the habit of breathing deeply and regularly.

***"I breathe deeply and regularly."***

## December 29: Mental Advantage

Perception is reality in the mental game. At a deep level, if we believe we are mentally tough, then we either have a mental advantage now or will have a mental advantage in the near future. Belief precedes improved performance. It rarely works that our performance magically improves without a shift in our beliefs about ourself. The key, however, is to believe in ourself at a deep level, the level of our sanctuary. Start believing in your mental toughness today by regularly meditating in your sanctuary.

***"I'm mentally tough."***

## December 30: Loving Challenges

As we advance in skill and competition, there are always new challenges to embrace. The challenges never end. We can use challenges to help us raise the level of our play. Mentally tough players love challenges. They know they help them improve.

There's a difference between accepting challenges and loving challenges. When we accept challenges, we view them coming from an outside force. We accept them and deal with them.

When we love challenges, we see them as being a way for us to learn to perform our best. We see the challenges as being fuel for our inner fires of mental toughness.

***"I love challenges."***

## December 31: Mentally Tougher

Imagine in the near or distant future, you've come to believe fully in your ability as a golfer and competitor. Imagine how you would practice. Imagine how you carry yourself as you get ready for competitions. Imagine how you would feel. Imagine how you would feel in the midst of competition. Imagine how you would look, how you would move, and how you would play.

Imagine playing to your highest potential and enjoying all the steps along the way that got you to where you wanted to be. Imagine you feel satisfied completely with the role that golf has played in your life. Imagine you're fully appreciative of the opportunities that you have in life and golf. Imagine you're mentally tough and enjoying golf more each day.

***"I'm always capable of being and doing more."***

# *Meditation Scripts*

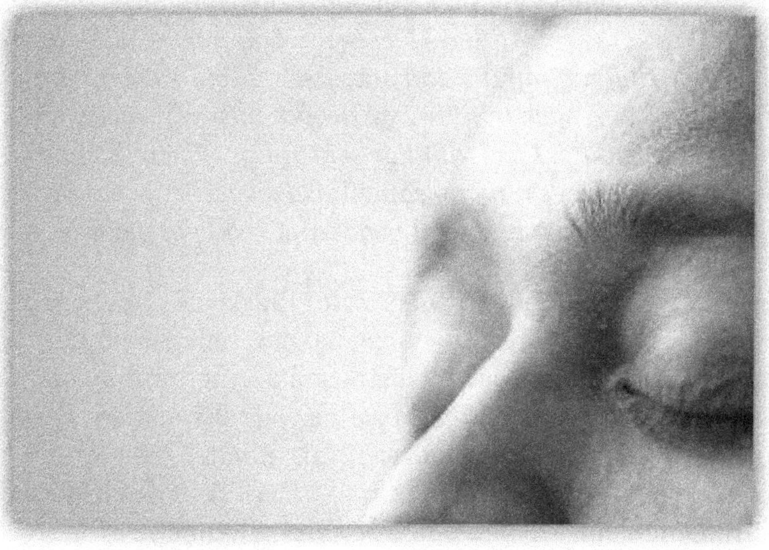

Use the following scripts with the meditations to have some variety in the meditation techniques that you use. The sanctuary is the core meditative technique, but we can use it in combination with other scripts. It's a good practice always to do your meditations from your sanctuary.

Always meditate sitting or lying down, in a quiet place where you can close your eyes and give your full attention to your meditation. Never do anything else that requires your attention while meditating.

## Sanctuary Script

Slowly say the following words in the script aloud, paying attention to the sounds of the words as you say them. Have the words make pictures and movies in your imagination, as you feel emotions and physical sensations in your body. You'll know you're meditating effectively when the words start to engage your imagination.

"*Deep meditation happens rapidly.* (Take two slow, deep breaths.) *With each breath, I feel relaxation spreading over my body. That same relaxation I feel in my body, now drifts to my mind, relaxing my mind. I can now feel myself entering my sanctuary. With each breath, I go deeper into my sanctuary. I see familiar sights. I feel familiar sensations. I hear familiar sounds. I travel freely in my sanctuary, wherever I want to go. I now relax completely. I'm at peace and ready to meditate.*"

Now slowly repeat your affirmation for the day, while engaging your imagination to make pictures, movies, sensations, and emotions. If you find yourself distracted during your meditation, gently bring yourself back to repeating your affirmation. Keep slowly repeating your affirmation for 10 minutes. You can set a timer to know when 10 minutes have passed. You can listen to instrumental music if you find that helpful. When you finish meditating on your affirmation, say the following words aloud.

"*Each time I go to my sanctuary and meditate, I find more benefit. I notice the positive improvements that I'm making from taking a few minutes per day devoted to my development. As I'm finishing this meditation, I'm feeling refreshed and ready to go. I will continue to feel great for the remainder of the day* (or *night*)."

When you finish, take a few deep breaths, and stretch your muscles as you give yourself as much time as you need to feel refreshed and ready to go on with the rest of your day or night.

## Designing Your Sanctuary

In the Introduction, we introduced the sanctuary and a process for designing your sanctuary. This script is an alternative way of designing your sanctuary. With this script, you design your sanctuary by meditating on one simple affirmation during a 10-minute meditation session.

To begin the meditation, find a quiet, peaceful place to sit or lie down. Close your eyes and take a deep breath, while relaxing your body. Then take a deep breath and relax your mind in the same way. Then take another deep breath and imagine going into your sanctuary, to your ideal retreat place. Then you'll slowly repeat one of the affirmations below for 10 minutes, having your imagination take you where you need to go. If you find yourself distracted during your meditation, gently bring yourself back to slowly repeating your affirmation. You can set a timer to know when 10 minutes have passed. You can listen to instrumental music if you find that helpful.

After meditating for 10 minutes, take a few deep breaths, and stretch your muscles as you give yourself as much time as you need to feel refreshed and ready to go on with the rest of your day or night.

The following is a list of the affirmations for building your sanctuary. You can add any additional spaces you want by creating your own affirmations. Use only one affirmation for each meditation session. You want to allow your imagination enough time to explore and create the spaces in your sanctuary.

- I live in a magical house in my sanctuary.
- I have magnificent short-game practice areas.
- I have a perfect practice range.
- I have spectacular golf courses to practice and play.
- I meditate in peaceful, powerful places.
- I relax completely in my sanctuary.

- I sleep deeply and peacefully in my sanctuary.
- I feel myself being healthy.
- I live a healthy lifestyle.
- I have great relationships.
- I have a magnificent movie theater.
- I travel to any place and time in my sanctuary.
- I'm the active person that I want to be.
- There are beautiful places for me to exercise.
- There are magnificent places to hike and explore.
- I have wonderful places to think.
- I see my future in my sanctuary.
- I see my past in my sanctuary.
- My imagination is lively in my sanctuary.
- My analytical mind quiets down when I'm in my sanctuary.
- I understand my dreams.
- I'm a free spirit in my sanctuary.
- I find my Higher Power in my sanctuary.
- I find holy places in my sanctuary.
- My sanctuary has magical places.
- I can be anyone I want to be in my sanctuary.
- I'm fit and healthy in my sanctuary.
- I have magnificent spa facilities.
- I have places of health and healing.
- I can talk with anyone I want in my sanctuary.
- I'm peaceful.
- I take care of my spirit in my sanctuary.
- I'm confident.
- I feel motivated.
- There are perfect places for me to have a retreat.
- There are places for me to let go of whatever is on my mind.
- I relax fully in my sanctuary.
- I have community in my sanctuary.

## Breathing Into Your Body

A common yoga practice is to "breathe into" things. To breathe into something is to have an intention and combine that with our physical breathing. As you prepare to do your meditation for the day, breathe relaxation into any parts of your body that don't feel relaxed. If there's a part of your body that often carries tension in it, breathe relaxation into that part of your body. Take a deep breath and imagine your breath bringing relaxation to the part of your body that's tense. Keep breathing relaxation into your body until you feel your whole body relax. If you feel your whole body relaxed already, breathe even more relaxation into it.

Now slowly repeat your affirmation for the day, while engaging your imagination to make pictures, movies, sensations, and emotions. If you find yourself distracted during your meditation, gently bring yourself back to repeating your affirmation. Keep slowly repeating your affirmation for 10 minutes. You can set a timer to know when 10 minutes have passed. You can listen to instrumental music if you find that helpful.

When you finish, take a few deep breaths, and stretch your muscles as you give yourself as much time as you need to feel refreshed and ready to go on with the rest of your day or night.

## Breathing Your Meditation

Go to the part of your sanctuary where you normally meditate. Relax your body by breathing relaxation into it with a few deep, slow breaths. Relax your mind by breathing relaxation into it with a few deep, slow breaths.

Now slowly repeat your affirmation for the day, while engaging your imagination to make pictures, movies, sensations, and emotions. Each time you say your affirmation, take a deep breath, and feel your affirmation going deeply into your mind, body, and spirit. If you find yourself distracted during your meditation, gently bring yourself back to repeating your affirmation. Keep slowly repeating your affirmation for 10 minutes. You can set a timer to know when 10 minutes have passed. You can listen to instrumental music if you find that helpful.

When you finish, take a few deep breaths, and stretch your muscles as you give yourself as much time as you need to feel refreshed and ready to go on with the rest of your day or night.

## Staying With Relaxation

Sit in a comfortable chair with your back supported. Effortlessly focus your attention on a spot on the wall opposite you, slightly above eye level. Take three deep, slow breaths. As you inhale your third breath, hold it for a few seconds before you exhale. Close your eyes and go to your sanctuary, to a place where you fully relax.

You can relax even more by counting down slowly from 25 to 1. As you count down, imagine seeing the number in front of you, and then erasing it. If you don't see the number clearly, just imagine that you do. With each number, you relax even more.

After you finish counting down the numbers, slowly repeat your affirmation for the day, while engaging your imagination to make pictures, movies, sensations, and emotions. If you find yourself distracted during your meditation, gently bring yourself back to repeating your affirmation. Keep slowly repeating your affirmation for 10 minutes. You can set a timer to know when 10 minutes have passed. You can listen to instrumental music if you find that helpful.

When you finish, take a few deep breaths, and stretch your muscles as you give yourself all the time you need to feel refreshed and ready to go on with the rest of your day or night.

## Relaxing Into Meditation

Go into your sanctuary to a place where you feel that your body will relax entirely. It may be in a spa within your sanctuary. You may be sitting by the ocean. It can be wherever you feel your body will relax.

With this technique, you focus on relaxing your body and letting all tension go. You do that by focusing on different body parts and relaxing them. You relax your body from head to toe.

Begin by relaxing the muscles in your scalp and then the muscles of your face, particularly your eye muscles and mouth muscles. Then relax your neck, shoulders, arms, hands, and fingers. Then relax your chest, stomach, back, and hips. Then relax your thighs, hamstrings, calves, ankles, feet, and toes. Have all tension flow out of your body. This technique should take a minute or two, but you can take as long as you desire.

After you've relaxed your body, slowly repeat your affirmation for the day, while engaging your imagination to make pictures, movies, sensations, and emotions. If you find yourself distracted during your meditation, gently bring yourself back to repeating your affirmation. Keep slowly repeating your affirmation for 10 minutes. You can set a timer to know when 10 minutes have passed. You can listen to instrumental music if you find that helpful.

When you finish, take a few deep breaths, and stretch your muscles as you give yourself all the time you need to feel refreshed and ready to go on with the rest of your day or night.

## Deepening Relaxation

Go to a place in your sanctuary where you feel your mind will relax and let go for a while. You might go to a waterfall or garden—to a setting that engages your senses.

With this technique, you relax the analytical part of your mind in a similar way in which you relax your body. Begin by slowly counting down from 299. With each number, relax even more. With each number, your mind quiets itself. Perhaps before you reach 280, your mind is quiet and relaxed, and the numbers disappear. You can also make the numbers disappear simply by relaxing your mind even more. If you count down to 199, then relax the numbers out of your mind at that point. Just let them go.

After you've relaxed your mind, slowly repeat your affirmation for the day, while engaging your imagination to make pictures, movies, sensations, and emotions. If you find yourself distracted during your meditation, gently bring yourself back to repeating your affirmation. Keep slowly repeating your affirmation for 10 minutes. You can set a timer to know when 10 minutes have passed. You can listen to instrumental music if you find that helpful.

When you finish, take a few deep breaths, and stretch your muscles as you give yourself all the time you need to feel refreshed and ready to go on with the rest of your day or night.

## Daydreaming

Effective meditation feels like a good daydream. When we daydream, we're actively using our imagination. We see pictures and movies in our mind. We're aware of our emotions and senses.

Go to a place in your sanctuary where you feel daydreaming is easy. Perhaps you like to sit on a beach or by a river. Perhaps you imagine yourself walking on a peaceful trail.

Now meditate on your affirmation for the day as you normally would, while staying in your peaceful daydream. Slowly repeat your affirmation for the day, while engaging your imagination to make pictures, movies, sensations, and emotions. If you find yourself distracted during your meditation, gently bring yourself back to repeating your affirmation. Keep slowly repeating your affirmation for 10 minutes. You can set a timer to know when 10 minutes have passed. You can listen to instrumental music if you find that helpful.

When you finish, take a few deep breaths, and stretch your muscles as you give yourself all the time you need to feel refreshed and ready to go on with the rest of your day or night.

## Music Meditation

Begin this practice by choosing some of your favorite music. The music should be uplifting and inspiring for you. Most people find instrumental music the best for meditation. You might use headphones so that you can fully enjoy your internal world.

Go to a place within your sanctuary where you listen to music and meditate. You might have an amphitheater or music room in your sanctuary. Perhaps you have your own music studio.

Start your music and let yourself drift into the music, hearing and feeling the music. You want to listen to and feel the music with your whole mind, body, and spirit.

After you've relaxed into your music, you can meditate on your affirmation for the day as you normally do. Slowly repeat your affirmation for the day, while engaging your imagination to make pictures, movies, sensations, and emotions. If you find yourself distracted during your meditation, gently bring yourself back to repeating your affirmation. Keep slowly repeating your affirmation for 10 minutes. You can set a timer to know when 10 minutes have passed.

When you finish, take a few deep breaths, and stretch your muscles as you give yourself all the time you need to feel refreshed and ready to go on with the rest of your day or night.

You can listen to a couple songs if that's all the time you have. If you have more time, such as on an airplane, you can listen to a whole CD. In this case, more is better.

## Walking Meditation

The purpose of this meditation is to become more aware of our body as it moves. We want to improve our ability to listen to what our body is telling us as we move.

Begin this meditation by taking a leisurely walk in a safe and quiet setting. As you walk, center your attention on different body parts, and notice the sensations in those body parts as you walk. See if you can give words to the sensations that you feel. Words give us a way of having a conscious grasp of the sensation, helping clarify our perceptions. Common words we might use to describe sensations are light, heavy, pressure, painful, sore, warm, cold, numb, tired, loose, stiff, free, flexible, lively, energized, or relaxed. See how much you can expand your vocabulary of bodily sensations.

Begin by focusing on your toes, and then the balls of your feet, and then ankles, calves, knees, thighs, hamstrings, bottom, hips, stomach, chest, lower back, upper back, shoulders, arms, forearms, hands, fingers, neck, facial muscles, and scalp. Focus on small areas of your body and see how refined you can become in your perceptions.

Once you've completed a scan of your bodily sensations, you can keep repeating the same process for as long as you want to walk.

When you finish your walking meditation, take a few deep breaths, and stretch your muscles as you give yourself all the time you need to feel refreshed and ready to go on with the rest of your day.

## Anchoring

Anchoring is a practice of connecting our imagination with an affirmation and physical sensation. Anchoring strengthens the contents of our imagination by connecting them with a physical sensation and affirmation. The physical sensation, affirmation, and our imagination can trigger and strengthen each other.

Go to a place in your sanctuary where you have some wonderful memories of you playing golf skillfully. Experience the memories vividly—seeing the colors, feeling the sensations in your body, and remembering the sounds and emotions of the experiences.

Now to anchor the memories, place your hand over your heart area on your chest so that you can feel your hand comfortably resting there. As you leave your hand there, say to yourself silently or aloud, "*I'm a highly skilled golfer.*" Have your imagination continue to focus on the memories of you performing well.

Keep slowly repeating your affirmation for 10 minutes. If you find yourself distracted during your meditation, gently bring yourself back to repeating your affirmation. You can set a timer to know when 10 minutes have passed. You can listen to instrumental music if you find that helpful.

When you finish, take a few deep breaths, and stretch your muscles as you give yourself all the time you need to feel refreshed and ready to go on with the rest of your day or night.

In this example, you've anchored golf memories, an affirmation, and physical sensation. You can anchor memories and affirmations to any part of your body. We chose the hand over the heart as an example. Experiment with various places on your body to find what creates the most powerful anchors for you.

You can use any affirmation that you feel is most appropriate, or you can simply use your affirmation for the day. After you've done this meditation a number of times, you'll connect the physical sensation, the affirmation, and your imagination. You then use the affirmation and the physical anchor to trigger your imagination to remember experiences and put you in the state of mind and body that you desire. With practice, you can learn to use anchoring effectively on the golf course.

# ***About the Author***

William Chandon, Ph.D., is a mental performance coach who works with golfers, athletes, and coaches to help them reach their potential and grow as competitors and people. He draws on his broad experience as a competitive golfer and athlete in many sports in high school, college, and beyond. He wrote *Meditations for Active People*; *Mind Games: Daily Meditations for Great Athletes; Mind Games: Meditations for Great Putting; and Mind Games: Meditations for Great Coaches.* He co-wrote *Smart Questions: Learn to Ask the Right Questions for Powerful Results.*

He has a doctoral degree in human and organizational development. You can reach Dr. Chandon or find out more at www.williamchandon.com.

CPSIA information can be obtained
at www.ICGtesting.com
Printed in the USA
FSHW022230141220
76901FS

9 781661 075217